GUN-DOG TRAINING SPANIELS AND RETRIEVERS

GUN-DOG TRAINING SPANIELS

AND

RETRIEVERS

Kenneth C. Roebuck

*Photographs by Ramon M. Rustia and
David G. Roebuck
Line drawings by David G. Roebuck
Cover photo by David G. Roebuck*

Stackpole Books

Copyright © 1982 by Kenneth C. Roebuck

Published by
STACKPOLE BOOKS
5067 Ritter Road
Mechanicsburg, PA 17055
www.stackpolebooks.com

Printed in the U.S.A.

Library of Congress Cataloging-in-Publication Data

Roebuck, Kenneth C.
    Gun-dog training spaniels and retrievers.

    Includes index.
    1. Hunting dogs—Training. 2. Spaniels—
Training. 3. Retrievers—Training. I. Title.
SF428.5.R585   636.7'0886   82-5667
ISBN 0-8117-0778-4   AACR2
ISBN 978-0-8117-0778-7

*To Joan and David with love
and to Paddy, who introduced me
to springers*

Contents

Introduction

THIS BOOK IS written for hunters who wish to train their own gun dog. I have confined myself to giving advice on the training of the flushing dogs, in other words the spaniels and retrievers.

I apply the description "flushing dog" to any recognized breed of gun dog used for upland hunting which does not point and is therefore required at all times to hunt close enough to its handler so that any game flushed is put to flight within shooting distance.

The eyebrows of the purist may rise at the inclusion of retrievers within the category "flushing dog," but flushing dogs they are, as proven by the many thousands of labradors and golden retrievers now in use in the United States as upland hunters in addition to, and in many cases instead of, their more conventional role as goose or duck dog.

I do not cover field trials for either type of dog, although some of the training I describe does in fact relate to that sport. My object is to explain to the amateur how to train his gun dog to a higher standard than perhaps he had realized was possible. Most hunters are blissfully unaware of the lack of control they have over their dogs, and appear to regard as trained any dog that will somehow find a bird occasionally within shooting distance. I have often heard the comment that "with a flushing dog you need to be really fit to keep up." Yet this is nonsense. The correctly trained flushing dog will quarter within shooting distance at all times and should be easily controllable.

Contrary to popular belief, one does not have to be the owner of a hundred-acre lot with varying cover conditions and ponds in order to train a gun dog. Access to such an area later, for advanced training, is ideal. However, much of the preliminary training in obedience and retrieving can be done in the yard or garden, and with surprisingly little equipment.

I know many people who would like to train their own hunting dog but due to lack of time and know-how prefer to have the job done by a professional. Others admit they have based their decision not to train on their own lack of patience. For those who do want to try however, a lot of fun as well as the challenge and fascination of learning more about dogs can be the reward, not to mention the pleasure of hunting with the finished pupil.

This book is also intended to help those who want to get their pup started and then, at the appropriate age, pass it on to a professional for finishing. If the advice I have given helps even a little in this respect, my efforts will have been worthwhile, for as any trainer will testify, the problems most dogs have when they arrive for professional training are invariably manmade. The first month or two is spent trying to correct these faults, which, had proper guidance been available in the first place, would not have arisen.

I have covered each stage of training in sequence, leading up to and including steadiness-to-flush-and-shot, an aspect of training often thought difficult if not impossible to achieve. It is a fact that steadiness is not easy to attain, but neither is it difficult to teach, provided each successive stage of the training towards this end is carried out correctly.

Keeping a dog up to standard once it has been taught depends primarily on whether your interest centers on your dog or on the hunting. The amount of enthusiasm you possess for dog training and work will decide how steady and controllable your dog remains.

I have purposely not laid down any strict timetable for training other than to classify certain of the advanced work as being for the second year. I have done this simply because all dogs are different, even dogs from the same litter, so to suggest that a schedule be imposed is unreasonable. More young dogs are ruined by people trying to follow a predetermined time schedule than you would imagine possible. Take it from me that a week-by-week training schedule, especially where gun dogs are concerned, is counter-productive in the worst way.

We aren't building a car engine or programming a computer, we're training a dog. And like human beings dogs differ in temperment, motivation, and intelligence. Some dogs learn quickly, others slowly, due to shyness and uncertainty. With the slow learner patience and persuasion are required, while the bolder dog needs firmer handling. Ploughing ahead to meet a pre-specified training deadline no matter what is a mistake. I cannot emphasize this too strongly.

I personally have had more than a few dogs brought to me by worried and frustrated owners who followed a laid-down training schedule to the letter. Their dogs, in most cases young ones, were nervous wrecks and proved extremely difficult cases to straighten out.

Time, in dog training, is of no consequence—unless you are paying a professional to do the training for you and are worried about spending too much money. The best advice I can give on training is: *A little at a time, and often.* Allowing each dog to develop at its own pace is the best way to approach the whole process.

Cardenwood Kennels
Copake, New York
1982

1

Choosing Your Dog

IT IS BEST, when consideration is being given to buying a potential gun dog, to select one from the breed which most pleases your eye. Also you must ensure, whatever your choice of breed, that your puppy is from good sound working bloodlines. It is all well and good having hunted with a friend's labrador or springer or golden retriever to be impressed by appearance, but you should also bear in mind breeding. In other words, inquire into whether the dog you're considering is from working lines or show and bench lines.

I must reiterate that I think it advisable to make your choice from the breed you prefer the looks of, provided the dog is going to be suitable for the type of hunting you do. You hope to have your dog for a considerable number of years to come, so surely this is preferable to choosing a dog for working ability alone. Having decided on your choice of breed, take your time and ask and look around. Do not be tempted to get a puppy from the first litter you see advertised. Enquire into the background of any and all dogs you consider. Ask the breeder right at the outset whether his pups are from hunting bloodlines, and do not commit yourself further until you have seen a four- or five-generation copy of the pedigrees of both sire and dam. Any awards shown in the pedigrees will be your first and likely as not best indications of a dog's mettle. For instance, if the awards are simply shown as "CH" this means the pups are probably bred mainly from show and bench lines as the letters "CH" indicate "Show Champion." The awards "FCH" or "AmFCH" indicate "Field Champion" or "Amateur Field Champion," and there's a world of difference. Dogs from show lines have generally been bred specifically for that purpose *and no other.*

It is well to mention here that we are concerned only with the flushing breeds and not the pointers. Most if not all of the flushing breeds are registered with the American Kennel Club, whose awards system for both show and field are indicated on pedigrees in the way I have described above. Most pointers and setters on the other hand are registered with the *Field Dog Stud Book,* where the letters "CH" stand for "Field Champion."

From time to time I have gun-trained dogs that have been bred from show lines and they have turned out to be useful gun dogs, but for the very small number that do, many more fail.

The tendency over the years both here and in Britain has been for the show breeder to be uninterested in perpetuating the natural working ability of the dogs he breeds. The breeding and rearing of dogs for the show ring relates solely to appearance, color, construction, and size.

Among the retrievers, especially the labradors and goldens, dogs can be found with show breeding and at the same time a considerable remnant of good working ability. But again, this is increasingly the exception rather than the rule.

Some "Dual Champions" (field trial and show) have appeared over the years—but very few.

The most frequent faults found in dogs of show breeding are: (a) a lack of desire to retrieve; (b) a tendency, often due to highly strung temperament, to be "gun nervy" (not necessarily "gun shy"—the two things can be quite different); and (c) a downright lack of interest in hunting. It is therefore with regular monotony that show breeding results in disappointment for the shooting man. But unfortunately, by the time these problems begin to come to light, the puppy is six or eight months of age and no doubt loved by all the family. Who at this stage is going to be rash enough to suggest a new home be found for the pup just because he's not going to hunt for Dad?

Ensure from the outset that the pup you select is from the right type of stock. Your chances of success in the field will be the greater, and your chances of facing disappointment and frustration the less.

The best way to start looking for the right dog is to question the owners of dogs you have seen in action in the field and liked the looks of. Take a look at the dogs' pedigrees if you can, and see if the point I've been making about show breeding isn't valid. Make a note of the breeders' names and addresses. In addition, don't hesitate to approach a professional trainer. Most will help willingly. The trainer you go to for advice may not breed or even train the type of dog you're looking for, but chances are he will know someone who does, and that someone will be the second step along the road to what you desire. Secretaries of field trial clubs are also a good source of information and are able to recommend breeders who can help. The American Kennel Club in New York can supply the names of secretaries of clubs (but naturally prefer not to recommend individual breeders).

When you go to see a breeder and his pups, if possible take along someone who knows the breed. This way you will be off to a good start.

I have included four sample pedigrees, each of which relates to a dog we own. I have done this to illustrate the manner in which awards gained in the show ring or in field trials are shown on pedigree forms, a copy of which most reliable breeders will supply—along with the registration application—when a puppy is purchased.

The first pedigree, marked 'A,' relates to a labrador retriever female we call Chrissy, bred here in the United States. The awards listed are:

FCH—Field Champion
This title is won in open field trial stakes, in other words stakes

in which both professional trainers and amateur handlers may compete.

AmFCH—Amateur Field Champion

An award won in amateur competition, i.e. a field trial stake in which only amateur handlers may compete.

NFCH—National Field Champion

Winner of a retriever championship, an annual event in which all retrievers having qualified during that trial year in open stakes compete for the national award.

NAmFCH—National Amateur Field Champion

The supreme annual event for the amateur.

DualCH—Dual Champion

A dog which has become both a field trial champion and a champion in the show ring (increasingly a rarity).

CH—Champion

A show champion.

The second pedigree, marked 'B,' is that of Gleam, a labrador retriever I recently brought over from England. This dog is bred from solid English working blood lines as can be seen by the awards shown, which differ slightly from those on the pedigree of an American-bred dog.

All the awards have been won in field trials, which in Britain are for all types of hunting dogs: spaniels, retrievers, pointers and setters alike are run strictly on wild game (fur and feather) on the large privately owned shooting estates.

In this dog's case awards are:

FTCH—Field Trial Champion

FTW—Field Trial Winner

Usually the winner of an open stake, in other words a dog half-way along toward winning its championship.

Field trials in Britain are not separated into Professional/ Amateur status. Everyone, whether fulltime professional trainer or amateur enthusiast, competes in the same stakes.

Pedigree 'C' is again of an English dog from solid working bloodlines, this time an English springer spaniel called Bracken. The field trial awards should be interpreted in exactly the same way as those of the labrador (Gleam), as all I have said about the awards system in Gleam's case relates to springers also.

Lastly pedigree 'D' also is for an English springer spaniel, Suzie, who is bred from my English female, Briar, to an American-bred male (Jonell). Again the breeding is solid working lines on both sides, but in this case the awards shown should be interpreted (1) in the case of the sire, Jonell, the same way as for the labrador, Chrissy, and (2) in the case of the dam, Briar, the same way as for Gleam and Bracken.

It is well to bear in mind also that where imported dogs are concerned, any awards gained, whether in the field or in the show ring in their country of origin, will not be listed on any official pedigree issued by the American Kennel Club, even though the dog was, on arriving here, registered with them. This is simply because the American Kennel Club recognizes only those awards won in field trials or breed shows licensed by them. However all is not lost. Those awards gained for instance by a dog imported from Great Britain are recorded on the "export pedigree," which is an official document, signed and stamped with the seal of the Kennel Club in London, which certifies the breeding and registration with them (the Kennel Club) of the first three generations of the dog's forbears. Such a pedigree is vital if it is intended that any imported dog is to be registered with the American Kennel Club. After the registration is completed the export pedigree is returned to the dog's owner, as it is his property and not that of the registering authority. Possession of this document therefore will in itself ensure that the owner has an accurate record of those dogs which have won their championship abroad.

In addition, it is normally standard practice for the breeder (or

Pedigree 'A'

Labrador Retriever – US Bred.

'Ludworth Mighty Monster'

PARENTS	GRANDPARENTS	GREAT GRANDPARENTS	GREAT GREAT GRANDPARENTS
SIRE			
FCH.AmFCH Carr-Lab Penrod	FCH.AmFCH Paha Sapa Chief	FCH Freehaven Muscles	DualCH Grangemead Precocious
			Grangemead Sharon
		Treasure State be Wise	FCH AmFCH The Spider of Kingswere
			FCH Deercreek be Wise
	CH Ironwood Cherokee Chica	DualCH Cherokee Buck	DualCH Grangemead Precocious
			Grangemead Sharon
		Glenwater Fantom	NFCH AmFCH Cork of Oakwood Lane
			Little Peggy Black gum
DAM			
Tidewater Charger	Whiskey Creek Achilles	NFCH '68 NAmFCH '67&'68 Super Chief	FCH AmFCH Paha Sapa Chief
			Ironwood Cherokee Chica
		Whiskey Creek Water Lou	DualCH AmFCH Ridgewood Playboy
			Chief Jet Penny
	Many Happy Returns	NFCH '65 Martens Little Smokey	FCH Crowder
			FCH Martens Little Bullet
		DualCH AmFCH. Shamrock acres Simmer Down	Brodheads Bar Booze
			CH Whygin Gentle Julia of Avac

Labrador Retriever – Imported from UK.

'Sandringham Gleam'

PARENTS	GRANDPARENTS	GREAT GRANDPARENTS	GREAT GREAT GRANDPARENTS
SIRE			
FTW Westelm Loyalist of Mirstan.	Westead Sweep of Westelm	FTCH Swinbrook Tan	FTCH Palgrave Edward
			FTCH Beinnmhor Tide
		Angeltowns Chalcedory Donna	FTCH Sendhurst Sweep
			Little Angel
	Geantrees Cressida of Westelm	FTCH Berrystead Glenbruar Beau	FTW Fenfarm Berrystead Barley
			FTCH Strattonley Plover
		FTW Geantrees Joanna	FTCH Holdgate Willie
			Geantrees Spice
DAM			
Sandringham Glimmer	FTCH Sandringham Sydney	FTCH Creedypark Digger	FTCH Hiwood Dipper
			Creedypark Saphire
		FTCH Sherry of Riteabout	FTCH Glenfarg Skid
			Moorhen of Biteabout
	Craighorn Dawn	FTCH Glenfarg Dante	FTCH Hiwood Dipper
			FTCH Norham Blackie
		Trentlock Jet	FTCH Margerywing Stag
			Sarcumuale Amber

Pedigree 'C'

English Springer Spaniel - Imported from UK.

'Cardenwood Bracken'

PARENTS	GRANDPARENTS	GREAT GRANDPARENTS	GREAT GREAT GRANDPARENTS
SIRE FTW Piperadee.	FTW Theydon Style	FTW Gwibernant Glyndwr	Garwgarreg Socks
			Garwgarreg Hasty
		Theydon Bee	FTCH Harpersbrook Sammy
			FTW Breckonhill Brando
	Raikes Busy	FTCH Markdown Muffin	FTCH Rivington - Glenshaugh Glean
			FTW Ludlovian Diana
		Hestfell Kestrel	FTCH Pinehawk Sark
			Covert Girl
DAM Smut face of Marchamley.	FTW Hales Smut	Conygree Simon	Slam O'Vara
			Conygree Minnie
		FTW Breckonhill Brando	Breckonhill Buddie
			FTCH Breckonhill Bee
	Ariadne of Aramathea	FTCH Markdown Muffin	FTCH Rivington - Glenshaugh Glean
			FTW Ludlovian Diana
		Conygree Flora	Conygree Simon

Pedigree 'D'

English Springer Spaniel – Sire US bred/Dam UK bred.

'Ludworth Suzie'

PARENTS	GRANDPARENTS	GREAT GRANDPARENTS	GREAT GREAT GRANDPARENTS
SIRE FCH.AmFCH Jonell. (US bred)	AmFCH Eastwood Chip	FCH Denalisunflo's Dilley	NFCH Kansan
			Criffel Micklewood
		Denali Babe	El Toro II
			F-AN-W Inc
	AmFCH Gentle Fawn	Red knobs Clem of Runors	FCH Staindrop Hiwood Spider
			Hardthills Laurel
		Farwin Fawn	FCH Johnny Ringo
			FCH Julets Breeze
DAM Brackenhill Briar (UK bred)	FTW Hales Smut	Conygree Simon	Slam O'Vara
			Conygree Minnie
		FTW Breckonhill Brando	Breckonhill Buddie
			FTCH Breckonhill Bee
	Ariadne of Aramathea	FTCH Markdown Muffin	FTCH Rivington-Glenshaugh Glean
			FTW Ludlovian Diana
		Conygree Flora	Conygree Simon
			Conygree Dulcie

owner) of any dog which is to be sent abroad to supply the purchaser with a copy of a four- or five-generation pedigree in which such additional achievements as for instance "Field Trial Winner" are noted. This is called a "breeder's copy."

I hope the preceding pages have given the reader a clearer picture not only of how a pedigree is set out but also of what to look for in that pedigree in trying to determine from what type of lines any dog you may be interested in is bred from.

Beware any excuses made by a breeder or owner as to his, or her, inability to produce copies of pedigrees of both sire and dam.

CHOICE OF BREED

When deciding what breed of dog you want for a hunting companion, think first about what type of hunting you do. For the man who is strictly an upland gamebird hunter, with perhaps an emphasis on pheasant, it would be hard to choose a better dog than an English springer spaniel. Few if any hunting dogs face the toughest of cover so enthusiastically as the springer, and their ability as an all-rounder on both woodcock and grouse make them hard to beat. On the other hand, those hunters who prefer waterfowl hunting should of course go for one of the retriever breeds. Their ability to cope with rough water when fierce northerly winds are icing up both marsh and shoreline is renowned. Of course all the retriever breeds can be trained as upland hunters (which I want to cover in this book). I train many retrievers to hunt upland, and an excellent job they make of it too, although in general they are perhaps less inclined to enjoy bashing through the thorniest of cover.

The following is a list of the better-known flushing breeds. I have also made mention of several of the lesser-known breeds, the use of which, sad to say, has declined greatly over the years both here and in Britain. Among these lesser-known breeds are the welsh springer, the Irish water spaniel, the clumber spaniel, the curly-coated retriever, and the American cocker spaniel.

Two other breeds, the field spaniel and the sussex spaniel, are now so rare that those members of them that remain are undoubtedly of pure show breeding, and for this reason I have omitted them.

ENGLISH SPRINGER SPANIEL

The English springer is known to most dog lovers, but it is not often realized what an enormous difference there is between the hunting English springer and the show English springer.

Mostly liver and white or black and white—with an occasional touch of tan on the face and body, the English springer is the ideal rough shooter's companion. Anyone who hunts pheasant with some woodcock and grouse thrown in—and who waits from time to time at a favorite beaver pond for duck to flight—is well served by this breed.

A naturally keen hunter and retriever who loves to please. An ideal family companion with the kindest of temperaments.

Over the years most of the best hunting springers have originated from Britain (and still do).

LABRADOR RETRIEVER

A very popular breed. Usually all black or all yellow, with some chocolate. Has a coat of great water-repellent capability. A truly excellent partner for the wildfowler and, like the springer, of kindly disposition and usually very trainable. Capable of standing extremely cold weather, with water work his greatest love. Usually exhibits good natural marking ability when a bird is downed. A keen upland hunter too as a rule, but tending to lack the drive and cover-bashing ability of the springer.

A good all-rounder and family friend.

GOLDEN RETRIEVER

Long-coated with deep-feathered tail and legs. A handsome dog to be sure. Usually happy and mischievous of temperament and slow to mature. Goldens remain puppies until two-years-old it seems. A very lovable dog with kind eyes and a great spirit. Like the labrador, a water dog of great enthusiasm. Some claim that the golden is not quite as good a marker as the labrador, but I don't subscribe to this theory.

The length of the golden's coat can prove to be a problem, especially where "burdocks" are in evidence, so it is essential to have a good mat-splitter and curry comb in your equipment (same for the springer).

CHESAPEAKE BAY RETRIEVER

Less well known perhaps than the two retrievers already mentioned, but very popular with coastal wildfowlers in the United States. Chessies are a rugged dog, comparable in size to the labrador but usually a straw or dark tan color with a curly coat which is extremely water resistant, enabling them to withstand the coldest of weather and water conditions. The chessie is inclined to be a loner, not as easy to handle as the other retriever breeds, a dog often with a mind of its own. It has a great heart and the wildest enthusiasm for its work but can often prove obstinate when training is attempted on stopping to whistle and hand signals. Nevertheless a first-rate companion for the dedicated duck and goose hunter whose motto is "The worse the weather, the better."

One chessie that I trained for a good friend of mine was used exclusively as a grouse and woodcock dog in the Green Mountains of Vermont, and she loved her work as much as any dedicated New England setter.

FLATCOATED RETRIEVER

This breed is perhaps less well known here in the United States than it is in Britain. It can be loosely described as being similar in appearance to the Golden Retriever, especially in type of coat. However the main difference is that its color is occasionally liver but normally jet black. The flatcoat is a handsome dog and like the other retrievers teachable and kindly of nature. The number of registered flatcoats declined in Britain during the first twenty years of this century, as they were overtaken in popularity by the labradors and goldens. Interest has been maintained however by stalwarts of the breed in Britain, and to a lesser extent here in the United States, and some flatcoats are still field-trialled in Britain and used in the shooting field. They were a great favorite for generations with gamekeepers on the big estates and there are indications that interest in them is gain-

English Springer Spaniel

Labrador Retriever

Golden Retriever (Courtesy AKC Library)

Flatcoated Retriever

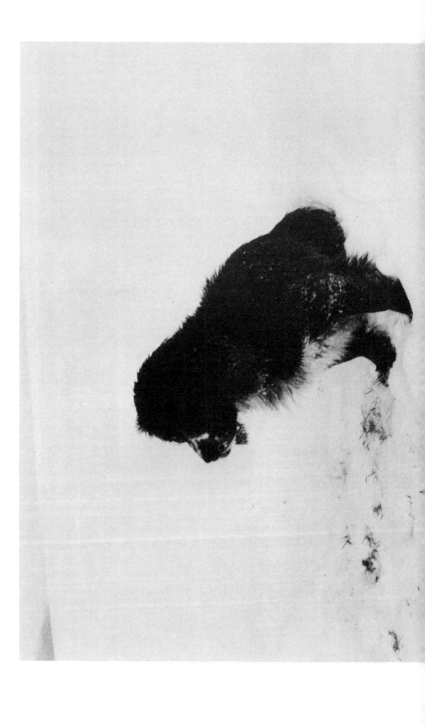

American Cocker Spaniel (Courtesy AKC Library)

American Water Spaniel

Welsh Springer Spaniel (*Courtesy AKC Library*)

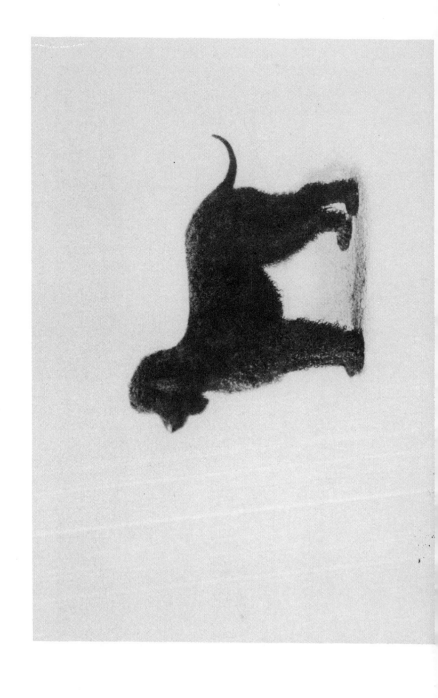

Clumber Spaniel (Courtesy AKC Library)

Curly-coated Retriever (*Courtesy AKC Library*)

ing ground once more. I have found them to be a pleasure to train and if more were known about them I feel sportsmen would be surprised to discover what a truly excellent gun dog they are capable of becoming.

ENGLISH COCKER SPANIEL

Slightly smaller than the English springer although originating from the same breeding (at the end of the last century in Britain, dogs from the same litter could compete in field trials classified either as springer or cocker depending entirely upon weight difference). Gradually the two types separated, and by the early years of this century they were permanently classified as two distinct and separate breeds.

English cockers come in a variety of colors from liver and white through black and white, blue roan, lemon and white, all black, and all liver. Not often seen as a working dog here in the U.S. but increasing in popularity again in Britain after a decline over the last three decades. Some truly excellent strains of working cockers exist in Britain and separate stake field trials are held for the breed. As an all-rounder from the hunting point of view they can be described as much the same as the springers with the reservation that they are inclined to display a little more individuality and hardheadedness at times. They are excellent cover bashers though, wriggling under and smashing their way through the toughest of growth. Their ability to handle cock pheasants and even very large hares is quite surprising. If from the right bloodline they usually possess natural hunting and retrieving ability, and prove good grouse and woodcock dogs.

AMERICAN COCKER SPANIEL

A smaller dog than the already small English cocker. Rarely seen out hunting any more, but a few enthusiasts still stick to what is now left of the old working strains—on Long Island in particular. A good grouse and woodcock dog and up until about fifteen years ago still represented in American field trials. Sadly, their numbers dwindled until there weren't enough among the field trial fraternity to make up a stake. The springers took over.

The Cocker Spaniel Field Trial Club of America still retains its prestigious title despite the fact that only springers run in their trials these days.

AMERICAN WATER SPANIEL

This breed, surprisingly, is not too well known by hunters. In size, the American water spaniel is similar to the English springer. However, unlike the springers and cockers, who have their tails docked, the American water spaniel is left with a full-length tail. His coat, like the Chesapeake Bay retriever's, is curly and usually dark-liver in color. The breed's love of water is unquenchable, and they can make excellent duck dogs as their coat is tailor-made for the job. Finding the right type of water spaniel may present some problems, but a stronghold of the breed appears in the states of Wisconsin, Michigan, and Minnesota. Two great friends of ours have owned several of these dogs throughout the years, and have worked them both on upland hunting for pheasants and coastal marsh hunting for rail and duck.

WELSH SPRINGER SPANIEL

Over the last ten years or so efforts to bring back the breed have been made in Britain. A Welsh Springer Spaniel Society exists there, the object of which is to cultivate interest once more in this very attractive breed of gun dog. The Welshman is orange and white, not unlike the Brittany spaniel, and I believe the effort to bring the breed back will be successful, allowed time.

IRISH WATER SPANIEL

The "whiptail," as he was affectionately referred to in his heyday, is rarely seen now in the hunting field. A certain amount of controversy exists as to his classification as a field trial dog, in that he is generally regarded as being more of a non-slip retriever than an upland hunter, and the few that are trialled here in the U.S. do in fact compete in the retriever field trials.

The whiptail is quite a large spaniel, with an undocked tail and a thick curly coat that is water repellent. A good working dog when from the right bloodline.

CLUMBER SPANIEL

Probably the least well known of all the breeds I have mentioned. I can recall seeing only one clumber being hunted (in England some years ago). The clumber is a large, heavy-built, thick-coated dog with a tendency to be ponderous in gait and a plodder while hunting. It is said that many years ago teams of clumbers were used by gamekeepers as beaters. The breed is said to originate from Clumber Park, an estate in Sherwood Forest.

THE CURLY-COATED RETRIEVER

Again something of a rarity in the field these days. Yet still used here and there in Britain. Years ago popular with the gamekeepering fraternity, and always regarded as an excellent retriever. Over the years the breed came to be accused of hardmouth. As the name "curly-coated" suggests, they have a curly or woolly-textured coat (liver or black in color). They were formerly popular with keepers not only for their retrieving ability but also because of their boldness and aggressiveness (characteristics useful to a gamekeeper sitting in the woods at night waiting for poachers).

Fortunately, a handful of stalwarts fights to maintain the hunting ability and increase the popularity of the less familiar breeds which I have mentioned.

I sincerely hope their valiant efforts will be rewarded.

. . . .

Choosing a puppy, especially one seven or eight weeks old, can be difficult from the point of view of assessing future working potential. However, you should by this stage have been able to satisfy yourself that the pups you are considering are bred from sound hunting stock. So now your choice is based on appearance. You will no doubt have decided whether you want a male or a female, so separate the pups, taking out of the whelping box or kennel only those which directly concern you. By all means be guided by the pup's markings, especially if it's a springer you're choosing—but more important than markings or color be sure to bear temperament in mind. Look for the puppy that seems bold and confident, that approaches you without signs of fear, shows interest in you, and does not run away afraid if you move suddenly or put your hand down towards it. Try clapping your hands and watching to see which pup is most attentive. A handkerchief shaken a yard or so away can often reveal the inquisitive pup who wants to investigate this strange new thing. On seeing the smallest pup, people invariably refer to it as the "runt" of the litter, inferring inferiority. "Runt" is a term somehow known to everyone, even those knowing absolutely nothing about dogs. But to reject the smallest pup for no reason other than its size is a mistake. Indeed, in my experience the smallest pup, perhaps as a result of being picked up and handled more because it is thought cute, is often the boldest and most forward. I can think of several smallest pups which proved to be excellent hunting dogs. I am not of course advocating that the smallest pup be chosen automatically. I am simply saying that to presume it is the poorest and least desirable merely because of its size is wrong.

Some people bring along a pheasant or grouse wing to try to assess each pup's interest in retrieving. This test is always interesting to watch, as most pups of the right breeding will willingly pick up and carry *any* light object, especially something as interesting as feathers . . . but the best potential retriever of the lot may in fact be the puppy lying around looking uninterested because of a full stomach.

It is better, in my opinion, to choose the pup that catches your eye, the one you feel you will be most happy to live with.

I fully believe that close human contact is vital, during a dog's first few months, and I therefore contend that much is to be gained if a pup is taken to its new home at seven weeks of age.

The question of male or female is one about which little advice can be given. I tend to find more attentiveness in females as a rule. But the choice is strictly a personal one—influenced perhaps by whether or not one intends to breed.

If a female is selected and breeding is definitely not envisaged then serious consideration should be given to having her spayed, preferably after her first season. This will eliminate the problem of her twice-yearly seasons possibly coinciding with hunting trips, and, more importantly, ensure that she will never accidentally breed and produce unwanted litters of cross-bred pups. Unplanned puppies are usually given away and often the recipients, because the pup was free, do not take quite the same good care of the dog as they would've done had they themselves decided to go out and buy one. The very least a dog deserves is a good home, and to risk subjecting one to neglect is in my opinion unforgiveable. Having a bitch spayed will not in any way adversely affect her desire to hunt, nor will she become overweight simply from having had the operation. Like us, she will become overweight only because she is eating too much.

So don't let these factors affect your decision. Stick to personal preference when choosing your puppy, and don't be overly influenced by advice from others unless you are quite sure the advisor really does know what he is talking about.

When looking over a litter, check to be sure they don't have runny eyes and note whether their coats are in good, sleek condition. Verify also that the dew claws have been removed (this should have been done at three-days old) and ask about worming and whether a follow up dose is required (it usually is). At least three wormings are normally necessary over a period of a month or two if you are to be reasonably sure that your puppy is clear. In addition to dew claw removal, tail docking should have been carried out at the same time for springers and cockers. Where working spaniels are concerned, no more than one third of the total length of the tail should have been removed (whereas show dogs are left with only a short stubby tail). Greater tail length, especially with a white tip to flag, shows up better when a spaniel is hunting, the tail action telling a story to the handler each time game scent is encountered.

Ask what shots have been given. Most breeders prefer that the owner himself take the pup to the veterinarian for the first temporary shot—to be followed a month or so later by the full DHL. Parvo Virus shots are also vitally important, now that this relatively new problem has appeared on the canine scene. I think it better if all this is done by the vet, as the owner can then see for himself that his puppy has indeed had the appropriate shots—

in addition to which he will be issued with a certificate to this effect.

In conclusion let me say this. I know one or two trainers who claim that when choosing a puppy for themselves they simply close their eyes, reach into the box, and take a dog out and go home. But for myself I like to take a careful look, bearing in mind the points I have mentioned on the preceding pages, then choose my pup and take my chance.

FEEDING

There are many good brands of "all-in-one" dog meal which fulfill completely the vitamin and mineral requirements for a puppy or adult dog. During the first two to three months after the puppy has been weaned, it is advisable to use a well-proven puppy meal and feed the pup three times daily. I prefer to soak the meal in hot water, leaving it to stand for fifteen minutes or so before feeding—but this is optional as this type of food can be fed dry. If you prefer to feed dry meal on a self-feeder basis, i.e. by having feed available in the bowl all the time for the puppy to help itself to whenever it feels like it, be sure to keep a close watch on how much is being eaten. Most puppies will regulate their intake and eat only what is necessary. But some, particularly labradors, have voracious appetites and will gorge on whatever is available. So if a puppy is seen to eat excessively, revert to the three-times-daily schedule. This will ensure a regulated amount, compatable with the pup's rate of growth, each feed. A careful check for a week or so will quickly indicate to you his daily requirements. Remember, he's growing, so feed him well and be sure there is always fresh water nearby. A milk supplement, preferably canned or powdered, (regular milk can cause loose bowel movements) should be given once daily for at least two or three months either separately or by using it to soak one of the feeds.

From about five months old feed twice daily. From seven or eight months feed once a day.

I believe in putting leftovers from meals in the feed. By "leftovers" I mean meat or gravy or green vegetables. All are good and are usually accepted and enjoyed.

Labrador puppies love to eat.

As for bones, I prefer not to give them either to puppies or adult dogs. Soft bones which are easily crunched up can sometimes cause a build-up and blockage of the intestines, which can lead to death quite quickly. If bones are considered at all, use only the large leg knuckle bones. These can be chewed and gnawed on but normally cannot be splintered. One of these sawn in half can keep a puppy or an adult dog happy for hours. They also strengthen the jaws and clean the teeth and are relatively safe if of the right type. Do not be tempted to give any others however.

Under *no* circumstances should you give a dog fish or poultry bones, as these can be extremely dangerous and could result in choking.

And above all, remember never to give one bone to two dogs, the reason being too obvious to need explanation.

HOUSE-TRAINING

For those who by necessity must keep their puppy in the house, or who regularly bring the pup from the kennel into the house during the day or evening, house-training is essential. The age at which a pup normally is bought or delivered—seven to nine weeks—is perfect for the dog to start to receive house-training.

In general puppies are clean. Even when still in the whelping box, when they want to relieve themselves they will walk to the end of the box away from the part they have adopted as their sleeping area.

I think it helps, at least until house-training has been effectively taught, to restrict the puppy to a specific and relatively confined part of the house—the kitchen for instance—because if he is allowed to wander freely, puddles will begin to appear. The kitchen is usually the best spot to limit him to because the floor can be cleaned more easily and thoroughly. A small fenced-off area can be arranged—for instance in an old playpen or a regular commercial wire pen of the collapsable type—the size of course relating to the breed of dog.

I suggest that it is better not to resort to putting down newspapers, as a positive effort should be made, from the day the puppy arrives, to have it relieve itself outside. To place papers in the pen will only confuse the issue, as the pup will in all probability have become accustomed to them in the whelping box, and will immediately assume they are to be relieved upon.

From the first day on, whenever the puppy shows signs of intending to relieve himself, whether by sniffing around rather urgently or turning in circles, pick him up and take him outside. You can be sure he will always want to relieve himself after eating, before being bedded down for the night, and upon waking up, so be sure to accommodate him at these times.

Taking him outdoors to the same area each and every time is a key to success. It is also a good idea to get him accustomed to a word of command which he will relatively quickly come to associate with this action. Any command will do. I usually say "Be quick," and believe me it works. When outside, by giving this command to the puppy you can have him relieving himself practically to order, and of course compliance should immediately be rewarded with praise.

Do not adopt a policy of simply pushing the puppy out through the door and then carrying on watching TV inside. He will start soiling the doorstep, in addition to which, if you do not go out with him you will not know, on letting him back in, whether he has cleared himself or not. Going out with the dog is the only way to be sure.

The timing of your pup's daily feeding can have an effect on how well he will last throughout the night, and a satisfactory schedule can eventually be arrived at through trial and error. If he is taken out the last thing before bedding down every night, he will very likely be able to wait until the next morning.

Once things seem to be working well you may remove the pen and let your pupil roam around a little, although by now you may find he will be inclined to restrict himself to the kitchen area (which may well suit you fine!). Keep a close eye on him for a while, and after a week or two you will probably notice that he will start to go to the door himself when he feels he has to. Watch for this tendency to develop. When it does, you can regard yourself as having won.

If accidents do happen, punish the puppy only if you can do so immediately. Otherwise, he will not associate any scolding you give him with what he has done wrong. Corrective measures such as scolding him or taking him outdoors immediately are effective only if you catch him in the act. And whatever the temptation, do not resort to the disgusting habit of rubbing the pup's nose in his feces. This is a very bad practice and may well lead to his starting to eat stools, as he must of course lick his nose to clean himself.

Remember, a puppy has a very short memory, and effective correction can be administered only at the time the offense is being committed. If you're too late then it's your fault, so don't take it out on the puppy. Just resolve to be a little more conscientious next time. House training can prove quite tedious during the first few weeks, but if you want an excellently behaved dog you will do the necessary work. Where early training is concerned, the amount of effort you're willing to put in—and the amount of your own time you're willing to sacrifice—are every bit as important as training technique.

SIGHTS AND SOUNDS

Allow a puppy to become accustomed to people and the sights and sounds of everyday life as soon as possible.

A point should be made of taking the pup out in the car regularly, and once you have introduced him to the leash and are satisfied he has accepted it and will walk happily along at your side, take him out and about with you. Let him meet people, children especially, and allow anyone who wishes to pat and make a fuss over him. Allow children to play with the pup in the house and yard but ensure they are not too rough in handling it. Make sure also that they refrain from having the puppy play tug-of-war with sticks, as this could lead to retrieve problems later.

Do not be tempted, as many new owners are, to try at once to discover whether your pup is "gun-shy." Do not take your puppy out and walk it along behind a line of twelve-gauge shotguns firing on a trap range. Doing this could and often does prove disastrous. "OK," you say, "I did that with my last dog and there was no problem." My answer to that is that you were very fortunate indeed and you almost certainly won't be as fortunate again. Introduction to gunfire is a tricky, complicated exercise which has to be carried out carefully and sensibly under the right circumstances (see Chapter 2).

Many are the strange and wonderful ideas held by some people regarding the methods to be employed in realizing their pup's potential. I was asked recently by the owner of a ten-week-old puppy if he should take the advice of a friend—apparently given quite seriously—that he (the owner) train his pup not to be hard-mouthed by inflating balloons and allowing the pup to grab them, thereby causing them to burst in the pup's mouth. Comment is hardly worthwhile other than to say that the mind boggles at such stupidity. The sad part is that the owner might well have tried it out had he not casually mentioned it to me first.

Your puppy should have plenty of running exercise, but always in your company. Let him off his leash when in the fields and woods, and as he gets a little older and bolder, walk him through the deeper grass and thicker places to accustom him to cover. You will notice the natural tendency of a well-bred hunting dog to want to use his nose to investigate strange and interesting new scents. Allow him to do this. It will encourage him to get into bird-holding cover and bash his way through.

Matters new and unusual are far more easily accepted by a pup brought up in the way I am advocating than by one which has been isolated in a kennel for the first few months of life and then suddenly taken out into a strange noisy world the pup has had no opportunity to get to know. For the sheltered pup the sense of danger and fear is magnified, and with animals of especially sensitive temperament a permanent sense of insecurity can be the result.

To get pups off to a good start I prefer that bitches have their litters somewhere where regular daily comings and goings take place, a porch attached to the house for example. I am a great believer in getting pups used to the clatter of feed dishes and the feel of human hands even before they open their eyes. You are then humanizing them without trauma, as they are all the while subconsciously and instinctively absorbing first the sounds (and, after two weeks of age, sights) of day-to-day life.

BUYING A TRAINED OR STARTED DOG

Although this book is primarily about training a young dog yourself, it will also be most useful to the owner whose choice has been a dog fully trained or partially started. The same principles of training apply and can be followed either to finish the started dog or in the case of the trained dog keep it up to standard.

Buying a trained or started dog can be a perfectly sound way of getting a good hunting companion. However, let me give you a word of advice. Never under any circumstances should you buy a dog supposedly trained or started without first seeing it worked. If asked, the trainer should willingly demonstrate to you all that it is claimed the dog will do. If the trainer or owner hedges or makes excuses about being unable to do this, beware. If it's too far away to travel to watch the dog being worked, then go elsewhere to make your purchase and do not be talked into having a dog shipped on approval unless you personally know the person selling the dog and have had previous satisfactory dealings with him. To do otherwise can result in problems, financial and otherwise, that you would not have thought possible.

Remember also to be prepared to pay a fair price for a good dog. Don't expect for one minute that any price quoted today will bear any resemblance to what you paid for "Old Blue" twelve years ago. Times have changed and so has the cost of living and trainers like everyone else have to try and cope. Months or maybe even a year or two will have been spent on the training process, so keeping down the price on a well trained dog is difficult indeed.

Furthermore, having got your trained dog home don't take him out hunting the very next day and expect him to perform for you precisely as he did for his previous handler. This is expecting too much. You must allow the dog time to settle down and accept you (and you him). He must have time to become accustomed to the newness of your voice tone and way of handling.

If the dog has been whistle-trained, try to get from his trainer exactly the same type of whistle that was used. A whistle of a tone different from that to which a dog has become accustomed can be confusing to the animal.

Above all, remember that a dog is not a machine. When you buy a dog you are not buying a new truck or chain saw. You are buying an animal capable of thought, affection, and distrust.

How things will work out is up to you.

2

Starting The Right Way

DO NOT BE tempted to try to do too much too soon.

It is important, especially during the early weeks, that your efforts be channeled towards creating as close an affinity as possible between yourself and your dog. The trust, response, and willingness to please that you receive in return will be the measure of your success.

The behavior of the dogs that are brought to me for training reveals instantly the attention—or lack of it—they received during the early stages of their lives. For instance, a customer once brought in two ten-month-old dogs, brother and sister. These dogs had been cared for most of the time by a manager who looked after the owner's estate in the South. To the manager, looking after the dogs meant feeding and cleaning runs. Exercise simply meant turning the animals loose in the woods for an hour or two to chase around and hunt on their own. Shortly after their arrival a litter sister was brought to me by a lady who had kept her pup in the house part of the time. She had taught her to come when called and to sit, and had also done a little retrieving work with the dummy. The difference in character and response between this bitch and the other two was incredible. The first two hardly knew their names. They could have cared less whether you were in the same field when out with them, and simply trying to get through to them that their object in life was to respond to and hunt for the handler was to say the least frustrating. "Self hunting" and lack of any form of discipline was without doubt the reason both turned out as they did. The other however was responsive and affectionate and worked with and for me at all times and was a pleasure to train.

Be warned! Where puppies are concerned you should start as you intend to continue. It has puzzled me for many years why so many pet owners fail to realize that if they allow a ten-week-old puppy to climb up onto the best furniture, chew on chair legs, and tear up bedroom slippers, the pup will continue to do the same as an adult dog. Walking to heel on a leash, if taught at three months old, quickly becomes second nature. The anguish of being dragged along the street by the same dog when a fully grown eighty-five-pound labrador is avoided. And yet how often one sees people being taken for a walk: a heaving, gasping dog being frantically held onto by an owner close to physical collapse.

So remember, those first few formative weeks of a puppy's life are a time during which the owner's influence can make all the difference in the world as to whether or not he will get the best possible response from his dog later. The admonishment command "No" is learned more easily at the beginning of a dog's life than at any other time, so use it.

The outcome, quite frankly, is up to you.

PRAISE AND PUNISHMENT

Sadly, there is no doubt that much harm is regularly done during training due to the owner's inability to "read" the canine mind. Insufficient thought is given to *whether* punishment should be given, and, just as important, *when*. An understanding of the principles of the psychological approach to training is crucial. In the first place it is essential to realize that if punishment of any kind is to be administered, the dog must know *why* it is being corrected, or else the punishment will have been given in vain. Take the common problem of a dog refusing to come to its handler when called. The owner keeps calling the dog repeatedly, getting more and more frustrated as his commands are ignored. The dog is chased and after much cajoling and persuasion finally returns, apprehensively, to owner or kennel. At this point the dog is seized and beaten and yelled at and nothing at all has been achieved. The owner has vented his anger, thereby relieving his frustration. He now has a terrified animal which is convinced it was beaten for the last thing it did, which was to return as requested. There is no possible way that the dog can be expected to connect the beating it received with its failure to return when called the first time. In the case of the dog who fails to return when called a check line should be used, rather than alternate cajolement and fury, so that the dog can be disciplined when he transgresses (see explanation of the use of the check line later in this section).

To be able to judge when praise or punishment should be given is crucial to successful training. The good handler will try to learn to think like his dog. Lacking reasoning powers as we understand them, a dog cannot interpret a command by hearing alone. The dog must be shown what action it should take in each and every exercise it is being taught. The trainer who, on giving a simple command to his dog, if not immediately reacted to puts his boot into the animal's ribs and yells incoherently for it to comply is comparable to the person who in an effort to communicate with a foreigner raises his voice.

Take the simple command "Sit" for example. In the beginning, the oral command "Sit" in and of itself does not impart anything at all to the dog. It is necessary, in conjunction with giving the command, to show the dog what is required by pushing the dog down on its haunches into the sitting position, at which point praise, both orally and by way of a pat, should be given. The actual word one uses to produce from a dog a predictable, specific response is irrelevant. Any word can be used to induce a dog to obey a given command, provided that when that word is used the dog is shown what his response should be. Repetition is necessary until the dog eventually begins to relate the command to the action. Voice tone is of major importance also, and a conscious effort should be made to give all commands firmly and quietly. Moreover, the trainer should vary the voice tone with each separate command in just the same way one does when giving praise or when reprimanding.

Effective and successful training depends to a large extent upon self-control on the part of the trainer. Control of temper is of paramount importance when training. Training should be cancelled for the day if there is any risk of the trainer's being irritated, even by a matter unconnected with training. The chastisement of a dog should in no way result from, or be connected with, a loss of temper on the trainer's part, irritating though the dog's disobedience may be. The trainer's temper must also be controled *while* punishing a dog for wrongdoing, as any sudden change on the dog's part toward complying and performing correctly must instantly be rewarded with praise, which of course involves an immediate change of the trainer's voice tone and attitude. Voice control, implemented instantly to denote pleasure or displeasure toward your dog, is essential . . . and without temper control, impossible.

Punishment should be short and sharp. I do not believe in beating a dog as I think little is achieved by doing so. My method, if the circumstances are serious enough to warrant it, is to pick the dog up by the loose skin beneath the throat and shake him, at the same time staring the dog directly in the eyes and orally chastising him. This method I think is far more effective than beating. A mother dog will correct her puppy by gently holding it down by the throat. An adult dog in a fight will attempt to overcome its opponent by doing just the same, except of course not gently. Domination in the canine world is enforced in this way, so it would seem reasonable to administer punishment along similar lines.

Punishment must be given at the spot where the offense was committed. For instance, in the case of the dog's failure to return when called, a thirty-foot check line should be attached to the dog's collar and the dog allowed to drag the check line around freely. If when being called the dog ignores the command the line should be immediately stepped upon, the dog stopped, and —most important of all—the dog quickly dragged back to the exact place where he first refused to comply with your command. He should then be shaken up and reprimanded, and the recall command and whistle signal should be repeated several times. In the same way, if having been ordered to stay your dog leaves his sitting position, he should quickly be taken back to where he originally was and corrected there.

There are of course instances in which punishment cannot be effectively given because too much time has elapsed from the moment the dog disobeyed. Despite your intense frustration, do nothing. Leave matters well enough alone this time, as more harm than good will result if the dog is punished too late. Far better to let the matter go for now and be ready the next time out so that you can react immediately and effect the correction in a timely way. You want to try to ensure that you are always in a position to see to it that your dog complies with any command you give him, so try not to keep shouting an order repeatedly if the dog is disobeying and out of control. If possible, keep quiet until you once more have him to hand. Then try again.

Be very sparing with any punishment, and before resorting to punishment of any type be quite sure that you thoroughly know your dog. By this I mean know what type of temperament he has. Do not under any circumstances presume that punishment of the type I have been describing is necessary for every trivial slip-up. It most certainly is not. Dogs with certain types of temperament *do* need such correction, but others of milder and more sensitive disposition may never need anything harsher than a finger raised and shaken at them combined with a gruff "No. Bad dog." Extreme care should be exercised with puppies under six months of age. Roughness should never be resorted to with them. The sensitive-natured animal can be quickly and easily ruined by unnecessarily harsh treatment. Encouragement and kindness are the passwords to success.

To review, punishment must be used sparingly, and only if it can coincide both in time and place with the specific offense being punished. The trainer should keep punishment short and sharp, speak firmly and quietly, and be ready to change voice tone instantaneously if the dog suddenly begins to obey.

Most important of all the trainer must be in control of his temper, since no owner can expect to control an animal if he has not first learned to control himself.

COMMANDS

The following eight commands can be used equally well with upland hunters or non-slip retrievers.

1. **Walking to heel.** Command *Heel* and point to left heel.

2. **The re-call.** Call the dog's name and command *Come*, or *Here*, and/or give several pips on the whistle.

3. **Sit and stay.** Command *Hup*, or *Sit*, and raise right arm and/or give a whistle blast.

4. **Marked retrieves.** Command *Fetch*, or simply use the dog's name as the command, and point in the direction of the fall.

5. **Unmarked retrieves.** First, stop the dog with one blast on the whistle. You now have his attention. To move him out to the left, command *Get Out*, pointing the way with your left arm. To move him out to the right, command *Get Out*, pointing the way with your right arm. And to move him out straight ahead, command *Back*, raising your right arm high and waving it forward.

6. **Hand over a bird.** Command *Leave*.

7. **Ignore the departure of an unshot bird.** Command *Gone Away*.

8. **Cease disobedience.** Command *No*. Shake dog up if necessary.

The following two commands apply to upland hunting dogs only.

1. **Casting dog off to start hunting.** Command *Hie On*, or *Get On*, and give a snap of the fingers.

2. **To turn the dog and keep him within shooting distance while hunting.** Two pips on the whistle, or whistle yourself, or

command *Come 'Round.* Give the hand signal to left or right as appropriate.

A LITTLE EARLY TRAINING

Puppies should be trained a lot . . . and a little. In other words, give your puppy many training sessions but keep each session short. Training should be of the simplest sort for the first two or three months. Early training should impart to the puppy the realization that when it is in your company, training is something it can thoroughly enjoy. That the pup is assimilating a limited amount of discipline and control at the same time is a matter about which the pup is of course unaware.

Exercises I consider to be useful with a pup during this early stage are: (1) teaching the pup to sit when told, (2) teaching it to come when called, (3) basic retrieving of a dummy, (4) keeping the pup within shooting distance during exercise (upland dogs), (5) introduction to gunfire, and (6) introduction to water (during the right time of year only).

THE SIT

This exercise can be taught very easily after ten or twelve weeks of age in or outside the house. Simply place one hand on your puppy's chest and the other across the back of his hips. Gently push down on the hips as you give the command. Do not force him down. Push gently on the chest and you will be surprised how soon he will start to respond by just the slightest touch on the back, which after a few days can in turn be dispensed with, and just the command given. At this stage, get into the habit of raising your right hand just as your puppy sits. This acts as a visual signal, the value of which will become clear in the advanced training later.

The most well-known word of command is of course the word "Sit." With spaniels however, the traditional command has for many generations been "Hup," which quite frankly I prefer. This command is firmer and clearer than the word "Sit," and can be given with more emphasis from a distance. Say both words to yourself out loud and you will see what I mean.

Using the verbal command "Hup," push down on the pup's haunches and pull up gently on the leash.

I use "Hup" all the time for both upland dogs and retrievers, unless of course an owner brings to me for finishing a partly trained dog already accustomed to the command "Sit."

I will therefore use "Hup" throughout this book.

THE RECALL

Most puppies will come readily to the owner when called, or when hands are clapped—at first anyway. When they start to become more inquisitive, and other things start to attract their attention—either by sight or scent—they may prefer to investigate the new and interesting rather than coming as called.

You should call the pup's name in conjunction with the command "Come," and if this fails, run away from him as you catch his attention. Chances are he will follow, as anything that is moving (yourself included) is far more interesting to a pup than something remaining still. If necessary, on those occasions when he seems to be paying less attention to you than to some diversion, call his name and the command "Come" and then quickly hide. Sooner or later he will notice you are missing and probably will panic and come looking for you. Two or three repetitions of this exercise will help teach your puppy to watch where you are and pay more attention to you. It will also help him to pay more attention to your voice. Every time he returns to you he should be rewarded with a pat and praise. Problems encountered with this exercise can usually be effectively cured by giving the puppy a cookie or a piece of his favorite dog meal. Food temptation is hard to resist and most pups will willingly respond when called if such a treat is in the offing. However, use this method *only if absolutely necessary.* I prefer not to depend on it at all, if possible, and would turn to it only as a last resort. Any well-balanced puppy or adult dog should return to you willingly and happily without the incentive of food if you have used common sense and patience from the beginning. Oral praise and a pat is all that a dog should require.

If reluctance and disobedience persist, consider having the puppy trail a length of light nylon cord ten to twelve feet long. The cord should be attached to his collar. He may at first be puzzled by its presence and attempt to pull it off or carry it, but very quickly he will come to accept it and ignore it. The cord will give you a certain amount of "remote control." By stepping on the cord you can bring your pup to an abrupt stop if he chooses to disobey. Then, having checked him with the line, you should repeat the command and at the same time give a gentle tug to get him moving back towards you. As he starts to approach you praise again must be given, while repeating the command "Come" two or three times in a quiet, persuasive voice. Do not be tempted to drag the puppy towards you. Just give a slight tug, nothing further. Do not overdo the check cord method as a dog very quickly gets to know when the line is on and when it is not, and, thus, when he must comply and when he can get away with disobedience. Perform the recall exercise at regular intervals, with the line alternately on and off, until the pup will come to you without hesitation.

If a puppy is taught the recall early, returning to his master's command becomes second nature to him. If problems continue to be encountered, however, then either the pup wasn't taught at the right time or else it wasn't taught in the right way . . . so take a break, sit down, and try to analyze where you went wrong.

The whistle can be introduced right from the start, in conjunction with the verbal command "Come." I recommend several short pips for the recall signal. You will be surprised how quickly a puppy will come to recognize and react to the whistle. The response to the whistle is often more positive than to the human voice.

INTRODUCTION TO RETRIEVING

For puppies, the retrieving dummy can be made from any suitable soft material. Stuff a sock with other socks, for instance, and sew shut the open end. Pigeon or pheasant wings may then be attached using strong elastic bands . . . but this is usually unnecessary, especially with puppies that are keen to pick up and carry. At first, throw the dummy only a short distance so that the pup can see it clearly. Remember that although you have started to teach the "Hup" command, your puppy will not at this stage remain sitting while you throw the dummy. He will run right in after it. So just restrain him gently by hand as you throw. Then release the dog with the command "Fetch." Keep quiet if he automatically returns to you with the dummy, speaking only to give praise as you actually take the dummy from him. I believe in keeping quiet if possible when a dog is retrieving, as this teaches him to return on his own initiative. Remember, later in life you will often be hunting in cover conditions which will make it impossible for you to see whether or not your dog has located the bird. In such a situation how can you give a command either verbally or by whistle? You cannot, of course. So during early training try to keep quiet during the retrieve. Allow your pup to retain his instinctive desire to make his way back to you with the dummy on his own.

With certain puppies this won't always work. And if problems are encountered by all means give the recall command and the whistle signal too, and if necessary turn and walk away to keep the pup coming toward you. In time it should prove possible to cut down gradually on the amount of encouragement you need to give the pup to cause him to return.

If while retrieving he tends to veer off to one side on getting

Keep quiet. Allow a puppy to search out the dummy by himself.

Try to encourage a fast return.

almost to you, counter this as before, by backing away and calling him. The chances are good he will follow you. If necessary stand close to your house door or to his kennel, as this often encourages a young pup to bring the dummy up to you more willingly. Also, for those last few yards, a narrow entry alongside your house, garage, or barn will help ensure a straighter run-in to hand the dummy over.

It is sometimes advisable with pups of sensitive temperament not to look them in the eye as they approach with a retrieve. This sometimes has the effect of putting them off so that they slow down and hesitate, resulting in a poor delivery. Lower your eyes therefore, if you detect any signs of reluctance in a pup.

No matter how much a puppy may be enjoying it, do not be tempted to practice more than four or five retrieves at a time. Finish while the pup is still having fun. Don't throw it any more that day. Puppies can quickly become bored as they, like small children, are short on concentration. Boredom quickly leads to faults which, once learned, are difficult to cure. One such fault is dumping and leaving the dummy. If your pup starts to do this, stop immediately. Leave the exercise for the day, no matter how strong the temptation to try just once more. You will probably find that next day the pup will pick the dummy up again without any hesitation.

I advise all my customers about this, taking care to point out the problems that overenthusiasm on the part of the dog owner can lead to. Some years ago I received a phone call from a worried owner. He had had his springer pup for six months or so and was genuinely perplexed. The dog had suddenly stopped retrieving altogether, although originally it had done so willingly. And the owner could not understand this as he had, he told me, thrown the dummy for the dog until *his arm ached!*

Keep a puppy enjoying what it is doing and you will hold its attention. Bore it and you are in trouble.

KEEPING WITHIN SHOOTING DISTANCE

Remember that yours is a flushing dog, and that when in the field it must at all times hunt and quarter within shooting distance, since obviously you want to be in a position to get shots at any game which is flushed. Bear in mind that this distance rule should be enforced not only when a dog is hunting to the gun but also when the dog is being exercised. A puppy kept within shooting-distance limits while having free running exercise will quickly get used to and accept this situation. The whistle should be carried when exercising the pup, so that you can get him used to the signal to turn back toward you (two pips, or the verbal command "Come round"). An occasional change of direction while walking will encourage the puppy to maintain eye contact with you and stay within range.

Don't overdo the whistle signal or the command. Only give one or the other, and only *when necessary*, as any command given too often may result in a dog switching off and ignoring it.

INTRODUCTION TO GUNFIRE

I think it would be correct to say that the two main problems created by owners with potential young gun dogs are: (1) retrieving faults, and (2) gun nervousness.

Introduction to gunfire can be one of the most critical early stages in any future gun dog's education. Done incorrectly and thoughtlessly it can result in problems which are sometimes extremely difficult if not impossible to cure. Getting the young dog accustomed to the sound and shock of the gun should be a gradual thing, done unobtrusively, while the pup is engaged in some other activity which it enjoys. Its mind is then occupied at the moment the shot is fired and consequently the sound is less likely to startle or frighten it. There are several ways of doing this, but my favorite method is the only one I intend to describe, as I believe it to be the safest.

I just mentioned that this exercise is best conducted while the pup is engaged in some activity it enjoys. What better time, then, than while a puppy is being given free running exercise? (I know of nothing that any dog enjoys more.) I take along with me a .22 blank pistol and while the puppy is running well ahead I fire a shot with the pistol behind my back. You may find that the dog will turn and look, or perhaps ignore the shot altogether, but whichever he does, walk on as though this new sound is the most natural thing in the world. Then, when the opportunity presents itself again, fire once more. With a well-bred gun-dog puppy of

Free running exercise is an ideal time to introduce a young dog to the sound of gunfire. Note that the pistol is behind the handler's back.

good temperament, this exercise will not cause trouble in the slightest. If the pup is obviously unconcerned, wait until he is just a little closer next time before you fire, but still fire with the pistol behind your back. Continue this for several days then try it out in conjunction with the use of a dummy for a retrieve, provided of course you have already started some dummy retrieving and your pup is enjoying it. Throw the dummy well out and time the shot for when the pup is at extreme range and about to pick the dummy up. Praise the pup on its return and then repeat the exercise a couple of times more. If all continues to go well try firing the shot as your pup is on the way out to the fall. Then progress later (if no problems are encountered) to a .410 shot gun, preferably fired by an assistant or friend well off to one side while combining the retrieve as before.

Continue with this exercise only if you are fully confident that your puppy is completely unaffected by the pistol's, or shotgun's report. If signs of fear or nervousness become apparent, stop immediately and proceed as recommended in Chapter Four (Faults).

INTRODUCTION TO WATER

The time of year during which a puppy is introduced to water is important.

It is quite obviously preferable that a youngster be taken to a pond or lake during warm summer weather rather than in late fall or early spring when the water is close to freezing. So if necessary, delay introducing a pup to water until warmer weather comes around.

Choose a place where the bank shelves down gradually and walk your pup to the water's edge to see what interest he has. Most spaniels and retrievers love the water and will enter it readily. The pup may paddle around in the shallows for a while, and on venturing further out will probably back off when getting out of its depth. Have with you a retrieving dummy, preferably of the waterproof canvas type that floats. Let the pup see you drop the dummy into the water only a yard or so in front of him, and encourage him to get it. At this point he may well swim right out and take hold of the dummy without further ado. In this event you should have no difficulty in increasing the distance by a few feet each time for two or three more retrieves.

If the pup is reluctant to enter the water, walk in yourself. Wear waders if necessary. Try to coax the puppy in. Sometimes an older dog which enjoys the water can be brought in to help, and without the dummy be sent in to swim in the hope that this will encourage the puppy to follow. This sometimes works. Failing all else, wade in again and carry the pup with you and *gently* lower it into the water. This can be as effective a way as any provided you use common sense and do not mistreat your animal.

Another method I have employed, when faced with a reluctant swimmer, is to attach a long check line to the dog's collar, then wade a creek, and having reached the opposite bank, *gently* pull the pup into the water if calling it fails. As the pup enters the water the pull on the line should be relaxed, and as he starts to swim across to you lots of praise and encouragement should be given. Done several times, first in one direction and then the other, this usually does the trick. Before long your dog should be jumping in with you and swimming over happily as you cross. Few dogs require this kind of treatment, however, and only occasionally do such methods need to be used.

I am adamantly against throwing a reluctant swimmer into the water. Such a tactic is completely unnecessary and can cause lasting harm. As in all aspects of training, patience and a little careful thought are the secrets to success.

3

Preliminary Training

OPINIONS VARY ABOUT when one should commence serious training with a gun dog. All dogs are different, even those from the same litter, and what the handler is able to achieve with one dog at age six months may be downright impossible with another dog of the same age.

I tend to find that with most dogs, eight months old or thereabouts is usually about the best age at which to start more serious training. This is an age at which you are able to put that little bit of extra pressure on, ensuring steadiness right from the start.

An important matter to be decided at this point is whether or not you want your dog, when finished, to be steady to flush and shot. Surprisingly, many hunters are perfectly happy to have their dog run in to flush and return with the bird as soon as possible. However, to be the owner of an upland hunter, especially one you have trained yourself, which is steady to flush and shot, or a retriever which sits unleashed and perfectly steady by your side while duck flighting, is to have a dog with that little bit extra, that final polish, which having been achieved makes any dog that much more of a pleasure to hunt with.

Your interest in having a dog trained to this standard depends largely upon whether you are a hunter first or a dog man first. Concentration on a steady dog is essential if you hope to keep him that way. You have to be one step ahead of him at all times and must be able to read his actions in order that your reactions and commands will be timely.

You must also of course be prepared to spend considerably more time, if you care to train your dog to be steady to flush and shot.

The training methods that follow will ensure an upland hunting dog steady to flush and shot, or, if the dog is to be used strictly as a non-slip retriever, steady to fall.

EQUIPMENT

The following is a list of training equipment you will need:

- A four-foot-long leather or nylon leash with choke chain.
- A nylon slip-cord-leash for the pocket.
- A thirty-foot-long check line with a leash snap at the end.
- A whistle, preferably plastic, with a neck lanyard.
- Two or three waterproof canvas throwing dummies.
- A Retrieve-R-Trainer (or dummy launcher) and two dummies.
- Blank .22 training pistol.

I think it timely to explain in more detail the purpose of two of the above-listed pieces of equipment, i.e. the check line and the Retrieve-R-Trainer, and to make clear my views regarding another piece of equipment, namely the electric collar.

THE CHECK LINE

This item of equipment is simply a light rope about thirty feet long with a swivel catch at one end to enable it to be attached to a collar or choke chain. It can be of use in basic training when for instance a young dog is being taught the "Hup" command, so that if he walks or runs away after being commanded to stay, the cord can be introduced to help correct him.

The dog should be walked at heel a short distance and then commanded to hup. The line, having been dragged along by the dog, will by this time be lying along the ground in a straight line. Walk away from the dog therefore alongside of and following the direction of the line (walking backwards if necessary in order to keep an eye on the dog), so that at the first sign of the dog's intention to walk or run away from you restraint can be applied both physically, by ramming a foot down on the rapidly departing line and bowling him over, and verbally, by giving him the reprimand "No" followed by a shaking up at the point where he should have stayed. The exercise should then be repeated until he begins to realize the futility of moving.

The check line, used as described above, is effective only if the dog moves away from you. This, however, is invariably what they will do in this particular situation.

The check line is also occasionally necessary when teaching a dog to quarter within shooting distance, and at times when training in steadiness to flushed birds. The line is then trailed loose by the dog as he is hunting, and meanwhile you ensure that you are advantageously placed to jump on it should the need arise, i.e. if your pup habitually casts out too far to the left and right, ignoring the whistle to turn, or if he breaks and starts to run in to flushed birds.

I firmly maintain though that if a young dog is guided correctly through each phase of the training outlined as follows, there should be little or no need for the check line at all, as a dog quickly learns whether or not he has one on. If the check line is used to excess and then removed, the dog will almost certainly take advantage of the situation by quickly reverting to its original wicked ways, knowing you no longer possess that magical form of remote control over him. In addition, when being trailed the check line has an irritating tendency to get tangled in everything within reach: the dog's legs, your feet, and seemingly every bush you come across. Check lines can at times be more trouble than they are worth and—I repeat—should be entirely unnecessary for any young dog correctly started.

One exception: training an older dog, one perhaps twelve

months old or older, who has had little or no formal yard training. This can present the trainer with a different set of circumstances altogether. You are dealing with a dog more mentally
mature, who because of lack of proper guidance when younger
has been allowed to get away with a lot, and in whom bad habits

A Canvas retrieving dummies
B .22 blank pistol
C Whistle and lanyard
D Check line

E Nylon pocket leash
F Leather leash and choke chain
G Retrieve-R-Trainer
   (dummy launcher) and dummy

and an excessive amount of independence have consequently been allowed to form. With a dog of this sort it may well be necessary to resort to the check line more frequently.

THE DUMMY LAUNCHER

The dummy launcher (or Retrieve-R-Trainer) is an invaluable aid in training both spaniels and retrievers, whether they are being trained as upland hunters or non-slip retrievers. The dummy launcher is used extensively both here and in Britain and is regarded by most experts as a valuable innovation. The launcher can be held in either hand while a specially made dummy is fitted to the barrel. A lever then opens the launcher and a blank shell, similar to those used in the .22 blank pistols, is inserted and the launcher closed again. By pulling back and re-leasing a spring-loaded firing pin at the base of the handle, the trainer can fire the dummy to virtually any height and in any chosen direction. The idea is that the report, followed by the ejected dummy, simulates a bird being shot and falling. Three different loads can be purchased—light, medium, heavy—depending on how far you want your dummies to travel. As they are waterproof the dummies can be used for water training also. They are most useful in teaching dogs to mark both single and double retrieves, and can be discharged by the trainer from alongside the dog—or by an assistant standing further out in the field. I find them a great aid.

Most spaniels and retrievers continue to enjoy working with the dummy launcher even after having experienced the most exciting activity of all, which to them of course is bird work.

THE ELECTRIC COLLAR

I have relatively little to say regarding the electric collar. In general I strongly advise against its use. The electric collar can, it's true, be used effectively to help cure some of the more serious training problems (those usually associated with the pointing breeds, rather than flushing dogs), but only in the hands of an expert.

When a dog has formed either the habit of *bolting* (bounding away to great distances while hunting) or deer chasing, the electric collar may possibly be used as a corrective aid. But it can be used effectively only by someone who thoroughly understands training and knows what he is doing.

There is no shortcut to training a dog well, and the use of an electric collar will not bring about any sudden and magical training results, contrary to what certain advertising literature would have people believe.

The use of the electric collar by the inexperienced trainer, who is after all learning himself, will almost certainly do more harm than good. There is no doubt that many potentially good dogs are ruined annually by the improper use of different kinds of electrical training devices. The training of a dog by humane methods should always be possible without anyone ever having to resort to such extreme measures.

. . . .

When carrying out any form of training, but basic training in particular, it is important that you first have your dog's full and undivided attention. It is therefore advisable to select a quiet place, an isolated field or yard or paddock for instance, where neither people nor animals nor any other distraction, including game scent, is likely to interfere.

WALKING TO HEEL AND SITTING TO WHISTLE

Either the leash and choke chain or the light nylon slip-leash will be used for this exercise. If you have already accustomed your dog to walking on a leash then the nylon slip-cord-leash will probably suffice. If, on the other hand, your dog pulls a lot, particularly if you are coping with a powerfully built retriever, then the choke chain will probably be required.

Walk your dog on your left side with the leash held across your front by the right hand. The left hand is for patting the dog when he is walking along correctly by your side. The right hand is for pulling sharply on his leash (in conjunction with the command

"Heel") if he fails to do so. Try to keep him walking alongside you with his head about level with your knee. If there is a tendency to pull forward or lag behind, give a sharp tug on the leash and *at the very same time (not before or after)* say "Heel." As he comes in alongside you and the leash slackens give him a pat and say quietly "Good Boy." Do not speak to him any more than you need to. Your praise of him need not be lavish. When you reprimand him, don't overdo it.

As you walk with the pup turn frequently to the left and right. Make 180° turns. So long as he is walking along beside you correctly, say nothing. Keep up a brisk pace, as any tendency to walk too slowly will make the dog walk wide or lag behind. You have already taught him to sit, so occasionally stop and give the command "Hup." As you do so raise your right hand and give one blast on the whistle. By doing this regularly you will soon be able to have your dog sitting down by either raising the hand or giving one blast on the whistle, and this is the very first step toward advanced training.

In time, but only when the pup is doing heel work well on the leash, you will find that the first stages of heel work *off* the leash can be started. First, drop the leash and continue walking along. Continue as though you were still holding the leash, and if your dog is still walking in good and close and sitting on voice-whistle-and-hand signal, try slipping the leash and choke chain off. Do this unobtrusively, if possible while you are actually on the move, and the chances are he will continue to walk along correctly by your side. If he doesn't, go back to the leash for a little while longer.

A useful bit of advice: Try from now on not to let your dog run free the instant you remove the leash and chain from him. Either make him "Hup" for a few seconds, or carry on walking with him at heel, leash free, for a few yards. If you do this conscientiously it will make for better control. Your pup will begin to wait for your release command (for instance "Allright" or "OK") to signify that the exercise is over and he can now relax. If there is any tendency at all on the part of the dog not to obey, do not hesitate to go back to square one. Reinforce matters for a session or two. Then, gradually, begin to build up again to the more advanced training.

Heel work with leash and chain. Note how chain is to be placed on dog.

Right hand holds the leash, left hand praises the dog.

Good heel discipline off the leash is important for the non-slip retriever.

Teaching the command "Hup" by hand signal and whistle.

I must mention here that where upland hunting dogs are concerned, a bit less time ought to be spent, initially at least, on heeling. This is because heel work, if overdone, can cause some dogs to become what is generally referred to as "sticky." In other words the heeling work may tend to take the edge off the dog's quartering ability, if both are taught simultaneously. I suggest therefore that so long as an upland hunting dog will walk fairly reliably off the leash, that for the time being is good enough. Heel work can always be polished up later, if necessary, after the pup thoroughly understands hunting and quartering.

Non-slip retrievers are a different matter. A good deal of heel work both on and off the leash is essential for any non-slip retriever. In the section on advanced training for retrievers I have recommended that certain distractions be employed, simply to test your control. For the time being however, be satisfied with your dog's performance if he will remain at heel off the leash while someone is clapping his hands and calling the dog's name in an effort to lure him away from you. Any extra time and effort spent in perfecting heel work with the non-slip retriever is well spent.

STAYING ON COMMAND

Before progressing to this exercise be sure that your dog has completely mastered the two previous ones on the leash, as it is important, if you hope to have a steady gun dog, that he understand the command "Hup" thoroughly and react to it instantly.

Commence by placing your leash or check line on your dog. Then give him the command "Hup." While he is sitting and you are still holding onto the leash or line, slowly take a step or two back. Invariably the dog will at first get up and follow. When he does, say "No" and take him back to the exact spot where you left him. Command him to "Hup" again, and when he does, step away from him once more. Perhaps this time he will keep still, watching you. But he will be puzzled as to exactly what is going on. If he does stay, allow only a few seconds to pass before stepping back to him. Praise him and repeat the word "Hup" two or three times. Repeat this exercise several times. If he continues to sit steady, back away further (still holding onto the line) and—

facing him—walk from side to side across the front of him. The least sign that he intends to move should be responded to with the command "Hup" and a raised hand. At this point, if you watch your dog carefully, you will see him actually thinking about it before he moves. If he moves, put him back where he was and repeat. Fifteen minutes of this a day for a few days should have the pup remaining when and where you command him to. Now you may drop the line and walk yet a little *further* away, always keeping in front of him and watching him carefully. (Lack of concentration on your part may cause him to get restless.) You will soon find that he will stay anywhere, and your distance from him can be increased daily until it is possible to walk both quite far away from and around him.

This is an interesting and relatively easy exercise to teach any dog, and with persistence and patience it really doesn't take too long to achieve. You will eventually be able to leave the pup sitting perfectly steady without the line on at all.

You may be wondering why I haven't suggested an additional command, such as the obvious "Stay," for this exercise. The answer to that is easy. "Stay" simply isn't necessary. If you have taught a dog to sit, then the dog is in fact staying so long as it remains in the sitting position.

One further piece of advice. Try to avoid getting into the habit of calling the dog to you once you have walked away from him and he has stayed. If you persist in doing this he will not stay reliably. He will start anticipating the recall. Every time you get a certain distance from him, and as you are turning, you will find that he is already up and on his way toward you. Calling him to you from the "Hup" position should be done later, once you are confident he has learned to stay. But until then *walk back to him* before allowing him to move, as this will ensure that he stays where he is far more reliably.

RETRIEVING

The original retrieving sessions were carried out mainly to assess your dog's interest and to make him understand right from the beginning that he must always bring things back to you. Now we can advance to retrieving practice to be carried out while your dog is sitting 'steadily' by your side—a consider-

Teaching a dog to stay. Hand signals should be clear and unmistakable.

If difficulties are encountered, a check line can be used to stop the dog from getting up and moving away.

able change from his puppy days when he was allowed to run after the object being thrown.

Take him out to your training area and command him to sit by your side. You can be virtually assured, at this stage, that if you throw the dummy your pup is going to break and run straight in to get it, since up until now he has learned the command "Hup" without being exposed to anything in the way of a temptation which would entice him to move. It will be necessary, therefore, to slip the leash and choke chain on the dog so you can exercise control at the right moment. Having done this, let the leash drop and, allowing for some slack, stand on it. Now—first giving the command "Hup" as a reminder—throw the dummy out six to eight yards. If he lunges forward to get it he will be sharply pulled up on hitting the end of the leash and will no doubt look quite surprised as a result. As he breaks say loudly and firmly "No" and place him back exactly where he was. Then walk off and collect the dummy yourself. The purpose of collecting the dummy yourself is to make your pup realize that from now on he will be allowed to retrieve only if he waits for your command. I tend not to be too concerned if at this stage a young dog tries to break because the correction procedure, if applied firmly and consistently, will quickly make him realize his error and have him sitting steadily.

Each time you throw the dummy be sure to pause and watch your dog carefully, not only to make sure he doesn't run in again but to allow him time to wait in silence before receiving your command to go ("Fetch"). Get him accustomed also to your pointing directly in front of his face towards the fall, but don't let him come to think that your point is in itself the signal to leave. Also be sure to remove your foot from the leash before giving the command "Fetch," as a sudden tumble when he has been told to go can be quite disconcerting and may result in a hesitancy to leave when ordered.

The object in waiting after throwing the dummy is quite simple. You are in effect teaching the dog that there is a distinct difference between the sight of a falling object (combined in time with the sound of a shot) and the handler's subsequent command to retrieve. This is absolutely vital. If steadiness is to be achieved and maintained in any hunting dog he must first come to realize that he can associate going to retrieve with one thing and one thing only, and that must always be your voice.

Never, no matter what the temptation, should you ever command your dog to retrieve the moment a shot is fired and the dummy (or bird) is falling to earth. If this is done often enough your voice will soon be forgotten and the sound of the shot or the sight of the fall will become the signal to go.

If all goes well, the leash can be removed after a time and, provided he still complies, the choke chain also. As with any other exercise, if problems are encountered when the leash has been removed, put it right back on for one or two further sessions. Training is a process to be taken one small step at a time.

It is good for discipline if at every retrieving session you allow your dog to collect only so many throws. If you give him four retrieves, intersperse these with two or three throws which you walk forward to collect yourself. You don't want your dog to get into the habit of presuming that every single fall he sees is automatically going to be his retrieve. Likewise, it is wrong for him to assume that the sound of a shot means a retrieve. To teach your dog this is to instill good manners. One day you may find yourself hunting with someone whose dog is also well trained, and in this event you will want your dog to know that birds shot by your companion are for *his* dog, not yours. Keep a dog guessing and he will always wait for your command.

Once you feel confident your pup will sit steady at your side, start getting him accustomed to your moving. Don't get into the habit of standing alongside him like a statue for fear that if you move a muscle he will be galvanized into action. You must get him used to movement on your part. So having thrown the dummy, step away from him a yard or so, or get out a handkerchief. And remember the point I have already made about putting your hand down in front of his head as though about to give him the command to fetch. Practice this well until you feel you have really gotten through to him. Then (and not before) you may start serious use of the blank pistol in conjunction with the retrieve. In addition to picking up the dummy yourself you should also fire the gun occasionally without the dummy being thrown. Not all shots result in hits, and your dog must learn to live with this frustrating fact of life just as you have to yourself.

Marked retrieves. The dummy should be thrown in full view of the dog.

Give a clear hand signal, pause, then give the word of command.

Amy takes off enthusiastically.

The pick up . . .

. . . a nice return . . .

. . . and delivery.

Buddy, a springer pup, retrieving from deep cover. This should be done to encourage a dog to use its nose instead of its eyes.

Cold-dead pigeons can be introduced to the retrieving sessions about now. Ruff, an American water spaniel, brings one to hand.

You may also start introducing your dog to some bird retrieving now. I recommend that he be allowed to learn on cold dead birds—pigeons being ideal—provided they are clean and not shot up. The training procedure is essentially the same as that for dummy retrieving. Most well-bred gun dogs, and especially those which enjoy dummy retrieving, will pick up birds right from the start.

Try to ensure, as with the dummies, that your pup makes as clean a retrieve as possible. Also be sure he doesn't mouth the bird enroute back to you. Any tendency to do so should be checked immediately with the command "No," and if necessary turn and walk away while calling the dog to keep him on the move. Mouthing the dummy or bird can be a manmade fault. Mouthing can be caused by stick throwing with the dog and then permitting the animal to go around chewing on the stick and dropping it at will. (So again, remember: No stick games!) Mouthing can also be the result of a loss of temper on the part of the owner when the dog was young. The dog might have interpreted the outburst as displeasure with his actually retrieving, rather than displeasure with his doing so sloppily or incorrectly. Thus, uncertainty has come to cloud the dog's mind as to whether his actions will be praised or chastised, and this in many dogs can lead to a slowing down and a hesitancy in returning, combined with a nervous habit of mouthing the object being carried.

I mentioned earlier that problems of slowing up and mouthing also can arise as a result of a sensitive dog's nervousness about dominating eye-contact with the owner.

Walking away from the dog the instant any sign of slowing up or mouthing begins—coupled with oral encouragement to "bring it on," etc., spoken in a kindly voice—can sometimes help matters.

Run away from him if necessary. Try to have him speed up and gently take the dummy or bird from him with lots of praise as he draws alongside.

If your dog lives with you in the house, some retrieving work with dummies indoors—no more than three or four retrieves at a time, remember—can result in considerable improvement. The dog is more relaxed inside your (and his) house, where far away from the field whatever nervousness has resulted in hesitancy and mouthing will with luck disappear.

When dead birds are being carried satisfactorily I recommend allowing the dog a few retrieves with live birds whose flight feathers have been cut (wing clipped) just so he knows how to handle them. If he seems startled at first by the fact that the bird is alive and attempting to escape, do not be concerned. Just quietly encourage him and he will soon make a grab for it and pick it up. After the first one or two birds there will be no further hesitation.

There is no need to overdo the bird work at this stage. The exercise is merely introductory. When more advanced training begins you will want your dog already familiar with birds both dead and alive.

Last—and by no means least—two points: (1) Endeavor not to get into the habit of carrying out retrieving training in areas with very short grass where the dummy is easily seen. Your dog must learn to use his nose, so choose areas where the dummy or bird drops into cover deep enough to conceal it from view. (2) It is a good idea, especially with any dog destined to become a non-slip retriever, to place three or four duck decoys on the training field beforehand. Your pup will become accustomed to seeing them and later, when doing water work, he will no longer find them of interest and will concentrate on looking for the dummy or bird to be retrieved. A dog introduced to decoys for the first time on water is not only puzzled by and attracted to them, but naturally at first presumes that they are there to be retrieved. By getting your pup accustomed to decoys early, on land, and throwing both dummies and dead birds into and beyond the spread of the decoys you've put out, you are preventing problems from arising later.

4

Faults

ANY TENDENCY ON the part of a potential gun dog to show signs of fear on hearing a gun being discharged is commonly presumed to be a sure sign that the dog is "gun shy." But very few dogs are gun shy in the true sense of the term. Gun shyness is usually an inherited factor. True gun shyness is apparent when at the sound of the discharge the dog takes off and runs away in sheer terror while ignoring commands or persuasion of any kind. Very few are affected so badly, but I believe those that are were born that way.

I doubt if anyone could give a really convincing explanation as to why the occasional dog is born gun shy. Those who claim to have cured "gun shy" dogs in all probability haven't at all. They have more likely than not cured dogs affected by "gun nerviness," which is a fault that is unquestionably man-made and which usually comes about as a direct result of employing thoughtless methods of introducing puppies or young dogs to the sound of a gun. Unlike gun shyness, gun nerviness usually can be cured by careful handling and by exploiting the dog's instinctive desire to hunt and retrieve.

It is assumed by many that if a dog exhibits signs of fear of thunder or firecrackers, gun problems are in the offing. This isn't so. If a dog exhibits signs of fear of thunder or firecrackers, the dog is scared of thunder and firecrackers, and quite likely nothing else. I cannot recall a dog which was particularly fond of either frankly, and in fact many gun dogs accustomed to sitting in a confined blind while a twelve gauge is being discharged four or five feet away can be terrified of both. Firecrackers should not be discharged in the vicinity of dogs of any age. Thunder, unfortunately, is a matter over which we have no control.

Any young dog will show signs of nervousness over any sudden loud report, especially one close by. Such an experience early in life is unpleasant. The dog's instinct for self-preservation will tell him to get away from the sound if it occurs again, so great care (as outlined in Chapter Two) should be exercised. It is far better to start right than to spend worrying weeks coaxing a puppy 'round because of something done thoughtlessly that should never have occurred in the first place.

The section on "blinking" in this chapter tells how to cure gun nerviness by bringing into play the dog's natural desire to hunt and retrieve.

HARD MOUTH

Hard mouth in any gun dog is a serious fault. The term "hard mouth" refers to the crushing of a bird during retrieving. I have known very few truly incorrigibly hard-mouthed dogs, but those few that I have come across have had mouths like bear traps. The result has been pulped and mangled carcasses with never a chance of a bird being brought back to hand alive. A dog of this type is quite worthless and should not only be discarded but most certainly should never be bred from. The least one should be able to expect from any dog, particularly one of the accepted retriever breeds, is that it will bring a dead or wounded bird back to hand in no worse condition than when it picked it up. All kinds of weird and wonderful methods abound which it is claimed will cure a hard mouth, but all these methods have ever proven to me is that sometimes—and I stress *sometimes*—a dog may be prevented from biting quite so hard *while the method is actually being employed.* Dogs quickly get accustomed to these little tricks in just the same way they get accustomed to the check lines and electric collars.

Hard mouth should not be confused with a puppy's tendency sometimes to handle a dummy or a bird a little roughly. Excitement during the early days of getting on to birds can be the cause of this, and the tendency can just as quickly disappear. I am a firm believer in not allowing any young gun dog to have pheasants for his first retrieves. Apart from the fact that they are inclined to be a large bird and difficult for a young dog to handle, it can happen that a wounded cock bird when being picked up by a dog will spur him in the face. Anyone having experienced a jab in the wrist from such a source will understand what I mean. Likewise being beaten about the face by a wing tends not to encourage a puppy, and either of these experiences could result in one of two things happening: (1) The dog will refuse for a long time to pick up another bird, or (2) The dog will put the bird down on the ground and kill it. And how will the dog kill it? By crushing the ribs across the back. He may then decide that this is the ideal solution each time a cripple has to be retrieved. Hence the start of hard mouth. Always ensure, therefore, that after retrieving dummies correctly your dog then learns how to handle and retrieve first cold dead pigeons and then live ones. Pigeons are a good-sized bird and present no danger when being carried alive, and I consider them to be ideal for basic training.

There will be times when a dog will return to you with a pheasant (a live one perhaps) which on examination is found to have either teeth punctures in the breast or torn skin at the base of the tail. This is not an indication that the dog is hard-mouthed. Damage of this sort can occur, for instance, when a wounded bird has fallen into dense cover from which the dog has had considerable difficulty extracating it. The dog has perhaps had to drag the bird backwards, by necessity holding onto the bird a little harder than would otherwise be necessary. So don't jump to conclusions too soon.

In addition to the hereditary factor, thoughtlessness on the part of the dog owner can sometimes contribute to a dog handling anything being retrieved unnecessarily roughly. I tend to regard stick throwing as a most undesirable action, especially when combined with the tendency of so many people to grab the other end and play tug-o-war. This is ridiculous and should not be done with any potential gun dog. Jealousy is another factor which can surface when two young dogs are playing together and the owner throws one stick, or one retrieving dummy, for both dogs. Invariably one dog gets the prize and the other tries to take it from him. The first dog resents this and clamps down harder with his jaws . . . so for "stick" or "dummy" under these circumstances read "real bird."

Common sense must therefore prevail with any aspect of retrieving practice. If you own two dogs, have them retrieve one at a time and insist that the dummy or bird be brought back to you and handed over correctly.

And tell the kids clearly and firmly, no stick throwing!

RETRIEVING PROBLEMS

A lack of interest in retrieving is rare in both the spaniel and retriever breeds. Most love to carry both dummies and birds. Remember the advice already given though—with training, a little and often is best. If you do detect a lack of interest on the part of your dog, try changing the article you are using for him to retrieve. Instead of the dummy try a handkerchief rolled into a ball, or your glove, or a slipper, or anything else in which the dog shows interest. If this does the trick, after two or three retrieves change quickly back to the dummy and often without thinking about it in the excitement of the chase the dog will pick the dummy up and bring it. Make much of him if he does so and conclude the exercise immediately. Then continue the exercise later the same day. If on the other hand your pup does not pick the dummy up, try attaching the dummy to the article he prefers. The chances are fairly good that he will eventually start taking hold of the dummy, and the original article can then be discarded. Another encouragement can be bird wings fastened to the dummy with strong rubber bands. Try reducing the number of wings gradually until only one is left and then try taking that one off. If that doesn't work, by all means go back to the bird wings, as this at least tends to indicate that your pup will probably pick up real birds without too much trouble. Live pigeons with one wing tied or the flight feathers clipped are usually tantalizing to most dogs, and very few retrievers uninterested in the dummy can resist chasing down and carrying one.

If you find you have a dog to whom dummy work is of little interest, but for whom bird work is a pleasure, accept the situation. After all, bird work is what the dog's ultimate purpose in life will be.

The tactic of giving edible rewards by way of bribery may also be considered, but only if absolutely necessary. As I made clear earlier, I prefer to avoid doing this if at all possible. If overdone it can result in the dog having his mind tuned to one thing and one thing only: the goody. And this in turn can lead to the dog dropping the dummy on approaching you in anticipation of the reward. Praise alone should be sufficient to encourage any dog worthy of being trained.

It should also be borne in mind that if your dog is not retrieving correctly, it may be because you have done, or are still doing, something wrong. Maybe at some time you chastised him for running away with or playing with the dummy, or worse still caught and hit him while the dummy was still in his mouth. Any temptation to punish a dog for wrongdoing while he is engaged in retrieving should be strongly resisted. He may well associate the punishment with the retrieving itself, and this could start him dumping the dummy when partway back to you.

When dealing with a rather sensitive or timid dog, try to remember (as I advised earlier) to avoid direct eye contact with him when he is returning. Direct eye contact can be intimidating to a shy dog, causing him to slow down or make a detour around you. Just lower your eyes as you talk him in towards you, backing away at the same time to bring him closer.

Lastly we come to the "forced retrieve" method. My advice is not to engage in it. If you have a spaniel or retriever that requires you to resort to this, then you have a dog not worth training. Get him a good home as a pet and start again.

BLINKING

This fault can develop slowly and unobtrusively and is invari-

Retrieve problems can sometimes be solved by having the dog walk along on the leash while carrying a bird or a dummy.

ably man-made. Blinking usually starts as a direct result of fear of the gun. The term "blinking" refers to the deliberate avoidance by a dog of a bird despite the fact that the dog has scented the bird and is aware of its presence. The dog locates the bird, circles it, and either carries on hunting or trots back to its handler, tail down.

Blinking is a fault which can be easily triggered off (if you will excuse the pun) and once started can be somewhat difficult to cure. Experienced trainers are quick to detect the first symptoms of blinking in dogs, whereas the inexperienced handler often does not recognize the danger signals, and, by trying to force the dog, only worsens the situation.

The dog that starts to refuse to flush is associating the bird with its (the dog's) dislike of the gun. The dog has reasoned that the bird is responsible for the gun sound, so the obvious solution to the matter is to avoid the bird. We have to assume that the dog was not in the first place properly introduced to the sound of the gun, and so, after giving the dog a break for a couple of weeks (no training at all), we start back at square one, start the retrieving exercises all over again and progress through each stage, but without the use of the gun.

Be prepared to spend several weeks on the following process. As you carefully move forward through the dummy and dead bird stages of retrieving, remember that patience is of the essence. In all probability it was impatience that resulted in the dog's being improperly trained in the first place. So however frustrated you may feel, don't ever try to hurry the training or depart from the tried and true principles you have learned.

When the dog is once more enjoying retrieving the dead birds you will take him out to the training area and allow him to approach a wing-clipped pigeon which is in clear sight and moving about. Circumstances such as this are hard for even the most sensitive of young dogs to resist investigating, and although he may at first be cautious and suspicious, in time he will almost certainly attempt to catch the escaping bird. After several sessions of this—and when it can be seen that the dog is going in confidently each time to catch the bird, substitute a flyer which has first been dizzied for the wing-clip. The fact that the bird now actually flies away should not alarm the dog, since by now he has had the opportunity to chase down birds that were flapping and jumping off the ground in at least an attempt to get airborne.

The next move is to have your pupil flush from slightly deeper cover, where the use of his nose rather than his eyes comes into play. This should cause no further consternation.

It is now, and only now, that you may consider bringing the gun back into things. You should plant a couple of birds out in the field before bringing out the dog, and this time carry with you the blank .22 pistol. Each time he flushes and is in full pursuit of a bird, fire a shot. The next time, having first planted the live birds, be ready with a dead one, and at the moment your dog ceases to chase the rapidly disappearing flyer, throw the dead bird high in the air so he can clearly see it and at the same time fire a shot with the blank pistol. The chances are very good that he will run straight to the dead bird and pick it up without hesitation. So be ready to praise him well. Continue the exercise for a week or two until you can see that your pupil's confidence is completely restored. It is only a matter of time now until you will be able to progress from the .22 blank pistol to the .410 shotgun (with a bird or two shot as the dog is chasing) and finally to the twelve gauge.

I have known the preceding method to fail with very few dogs, and those with which it did fail were discarded for hunting.

It will be noticed that I have advocated bird chasing as a means towards curing a dog of blinking. This, it must be clearly understood, is a means to an end only. A dog you intend to be steady to wing and shot should not normally be permitted to chase flushed birds. Allowing chasing to help cure blinking is done to build up the dog's confidence. You are using his instinctive desire to hunt and retrieve to overcome his nerviness. When you feel the desired result has been achieved, further chasing must be stopped.

Proceed very carefully with a dog in which you have detected the blinking problem. He may still not be mature enough to take the steadiness training. When anything untoward arises, stop and think. Try to figure out what went wrong. Invariably the problem will turn out to lie with the handler and not the dog.

work, can be allowed to retrieve over considerably greater distances.)

When loading the dummy launcher always load dummy first, shell second. When closing the launcher be sure it is pointing away from the dog. A sudden accidental discharge (caused for instance by the firing pin catching on your coat) could be pretty disastrous at close range, resulting in bodily injury and/or irreparable psychological damage to a promising young dog.

Before firing, be sure you have your dog's full attention. Repeat the command "Hup," then fire the dummy well out and clearly in sight. Pause for an appropriate length of time, then send him for the retrieve. Extra vigilance should be exercised when starting work with the launcher, as the launcher-fired dummy will be more exciting to your dog than the hand-thrown one, with the result that the dog will be more tempted to break. If any sign of movement is detected, reprimand him with the word "No." If he breaks, put the leash or check line on for the next three or four retrieves. He should soon realize that there must be no difference between his response to the hand-thrown dummy and his response to the launch-fired one.

The angle at which the dummy is fired should be varied to teach the dog to turn and watch the course of the dummy, and again, be sure to fire the dummy into cover sufficient to conceal it from view. Take notice of wind direction too, and endeavor to direct the dummy across the wind rather than with or against it. It is interesting to watch the dog pass downwind of the fall and suddenly check and turn. When he does this you know he really is using his nose rather than his eyes.

As before, don't overdo the number of retrieves, and pick up the occasional one yourself while leaving the dog on the "Hup." A variation on the use of the launcher can be achieved by having a friend fire the dummies from behind a hedge or bush. This can be done for instance while you are walking a retriever along at heel. At the sound of the shot and the appearance of the dummy the dog should be commanded to "Hup" alongside you. Then, after an appropriate pause, send him out for the retrieve.

If the fall is badly marked and your dog is working his way back toward you, walk out toward him and using your hand signal give the command "Back" to get him to go further out and away

Loading the launcher. Place dummy on first . . .

. . . shell in second . . .

. . . close the action . . .

. . . and you're ready to fire.

Having first reminded the dog to hup, fire the dummy high and well out.

Pause before giving the command to retrieve.

Most good spaniels and retrievers enjoy this all their lives.

from you. If he complies, keep quiet and repeat the command only if it again becomes necessary. If he continues to hunt persistently in the area of the fall, remain quiet. Unnecessarily repeated commands tend to break a dog's concentration. It is extremely important that his natural drive to keep on hunting should be preserved. Repeatedly distracting him may cause him to start relying too much on your assistance, which in turn will cause him to give up too easily in anticipation of help from you. Obviously in marshy conditions with high reeds or in woodland with dense undergrowth you would be unable to help him anyway.

And don't nag your dog. A noisy handler just scares game.

WATER WORK

This is an aspect of training which any gun dog, retriever or spaniel, thoroughly enjoys, and to be a success as an all-'rounder should be familiar with.

There can be few things more frustrating than to have a bird fall into water or onto the far side of a creek and to have with you a dog that either refuses to swim out for it or, having crossed the creek, cannot be directed up the bank to locate it.

I mention both retrieving *from* water and *from across* water. Each is of great importance. I derive considerable satisfaction from watching a dog doing water work on singles and doubles while being handled from the other side of a creek or narrow river.

To get started with water work, choose a pond or lake with a gradually shelving bank and sit your dog alongside you in just the same way you would for land retrieves. Use hand-thrown dummies. The first two or three retrieves should not be too far out. Let the dog demonstrate to you that he can mark a fall on water just as well as on land. Some young dogs clearly see where the dummy hits the water but tend to lose their sense of direction on entering the water to swim out for it.

I like a dog to enter water boldly, but I am no more impressed with a dog that leaps in than I am with one that enters slowly but positively. In fact I tend to prefer the latter, as the over-eager dog can get himself injured by striking submerged obstacles or by being torn on barbed wire secured to fence posts half submerged along creeks subject to bank erosion.

Try to ensure that as your dog emerges from the water he brings the dummy straight toward you without hesitation. Try to avoid his getting in the habit of dropping the dummy while he shakes. Hesitation to come straight to you on leaving the water may be corrected by turning and walking away from the dog as he reaches land. As you turn and walk away, call his name. This normally keeps a dog moving so that the dummy can be taken from him as he draws alongside you.

If he drops the dummy repeatedly, on the next retrieve walk into the water yourself for a short distance and gently take the dummy from his mouth while the water is still too deep for him to walk. Do this several times, then gradually decrease the distance until he is beginning to touch bottom, and continue until the delivery is being made clear of the water on the bank itself. If all is going well, continue to retreat a bit with each retrieve until he is carrying the dummy directly to you well back from the water's edge.

If he absolutely insists on stopping to shake and putting the dummy down as he does so (and with certain dogs there is simply no way to prevent this), at least be sure he picks the dummy up promptly after shaking and delivers it immediately to hand.

Also, practice sending your dog for retrieves from a position well back from the edge of the water so that he has to run a few yards, preferably through reeds, before entering the water. More often than not, especially when waiting for duck to flight, this is the sort of situation under which you will be operating.

Remember to use three or four duck decoys. It will be best in the beginning to place them in a rather tight bunch fairly close to the bank so that your dog will pass to the left or right of them on entering the water. In this way he will be closer to you and in easier control range, should the decoys start to interest him. Later the decoys may be situated further out. Arrange them in a more normal spread pattern and position them so that your dog must swim through them to make his retrieve—but space them widely enough apart to avoid his accidentally dragging one along by its anchor line.

For retrieving from across the water, select a creek with fairly low banks. This will enable your pupil to enter and leave the water without too much difficulty. At first, throw the dummy so that it lands *just* on the far side—and in clear view. The distance can then be extended yard by yard as the dog's proficiency increases. Eventually he will hunt well out beyond the edge of the opposite bank. As training progresses station a friend, concealed if possible, on the far side of the creek with three or four dummies or dead pigeons and the blank pistol. This way the dummies can be thrown out further still, and the dog is learning a further way of marking under differing circumstances. Gradually move back until you are able, provided he still has a good clear view, to send him from about twenty yards back from the creek. Move back only if he is progressing well. If not, stay still or even move forward a little until his marking has improved.

Once the dog is handling this, the dummy launcher may be brought into use and used in exactly the same manner as on land.

It will be possible later, once your dog has learned hand signals and direction control, to direct him left or right or further out while he is swimming. After his attention has been attracted by the whistle, a clear hand signal combined with the appro-

Retrieving from a pond. Daisy, a springer spaniel, makes a good water entry.

If at all possible, decoys should be used. You want the dog to get accustomed to retrieving from among them.

Retrieving from across a creek. Gleam, a yellow labrador, watches intently as a dead pigeon is thrown to the opposite bank.

The verbal and visual command signals to go are given.

Very cold water . . . but this is an experienced dog. Pups should be started when the weather is warmer.

Heading for the opposite bank in a fairly swift current.

The bird has been collected.

Back with the bird.

Practice on steep banks is fine for the more experienced retriever.

A nicely completed retrieve. Cold water doesn't worry an enthusiastic labrador.

priate command should result in his altering course in the desired direction. However you must refrain from beginning this training on water until your dog has learned hand signals and direction control on land (see Chapter 9), as any failures out on the water are most difficult if not impossible to correct.

An aspect of water work training overlooked by many hunters is retrieving from a boat. Throughout the hunting season the opportunity to hunt ducks from a boat may occur from time to time and steps should be taken to get your dog accustomed to it. Most dogs will sit quite happily in a boat once they get used to the movement. To help your pup gain confidence in jumping out, start the retrieves with the boat drawn up on land close to the water's edge. You may at first have some difficulty persuading the dog to jump from the boat into deep water, but patience and persuasion combined with the inducement of a few dead bird retrieves should soon help overcome this. Once confidence is gained he will dive out with enthusiasm. When he arrives back at the boat with the retrieve, take the dummy or bird first. Then help him climb in by grasping the loose skin at the back of his neck as he levers himself aboard.

Advice relating to the use of live birds for water work will be found in Chapter Seven (Advanced Training for Retrievers) and the methods described apply to the upland hunting dog exactly as they do to the non-slip retriever.

BIRDS AND BIRD PLANTING

It is usually necessary to resort to artificial means to give a young dog experience on bird work. Property licensed as a "Shooting Preserve" affords the trainer the opportunity (in many states) to shoot game birds over dogs for seven months of the year (September through March), which is of course a considerable advantage. The amateur trainer however probably has no access to such facilities other than as a paying customer, and the professional finds that the time of year when game birds may not be shot is the very time when his training schedule is at its busiest.

Gun-dog trainers in Britain do much of their early training in large fenced enclosures known as "rabbit pens," in which wild or semi-tame rabbits and often wing-clipped birds live freely amid natural cover and piles of brush or pine branches. In Britain rabbits were always hunted with springers, at least up to 1954, when a disease known as myxamatosis appeared on the scene (introduced from Australia) and almost completely wiped the rabbit out. The rabbit is a hardy species however, and has managed to survive in isolated pockets, even developing a certain amount of natural immunity to the disease. But the rabbit no longer populates Britain in vast numbers, and the spaniel's role has become more that of full-time bird hunter, with rabbit retrieves more the exception than the rule. As a true all-'rounder though the spaniel is expected to cope with any retrieve whether fur or feather, as is the retriever. And in Britain, days out hunting or field-trialling regularly result in a variety of retrieves (pheasant, partridge, woodcock, snipe, woodpigeon, duck, rabbit, hare, and so on). We are concerned here, however, with using spaniels and retrievers for upland hunting, with pheasants and grouse and woodcock being the main quarry. The occasions on which a rabbit is flushed during bird hunting are few and far between, so specific training for steadiness to rabbits is really of minor importance.

In training with live birds, birds have to be used which are not affected by the game laws, and the answer—especially for the flushing breeds—is pigeons. They are a relatively easy bird to obtain and sources include breeders who are reducing their stock or dealers who buy and sell in large quantities. Pigeons can also be trapped in farm silos and barns, where the nuisance they cause usually makes the owner more than willing to let you trap.

I prefer not to use quail from a call-back pen as they often tend not to fly far enough, and they are inclined to flush in groups of two or three—hardly suitable during initial steadiness training for the breeds we are concerned with.

I do of course use quail for the pointing breeds, for which they are ideal. Chukar partridge, which like pigeons tend to fly hard, can be good for the flushing dogs but are difficult to obtain during spring and summer.

In addition to being strong fliers, piegons are a suitable size for a young dog to carry, and, normally, if he will retrieve pigeons, little or no difficulty will be experienced when he gets into re-

Bird planting: the correct way to hold a pigeon.

Dizzying the bird by swinging it. Only a few seconds of swinging are required.

The bird is placed in the grass and in a matter of a few seconds has fully recovered.

trieving game birds later. As I have already mentioned, pigeons also present no danger to the inexperienced dog, whereas the spurs of a wounded cock pheasant can be quite formidable.

The use of pigeons as an aid in training your dog is essential, especially in the early stages of teaching steadiness-to-flush (after steadiness-to-thrown-dummies has been accomplished). Two or three pre-dizzied birds will be planted well apart from each other. (I'll explain "pre-dizzied" in a moment.) The dog can then be hunted towards them and on getting their scent be allowed to run in and flush. This artificial method simulates what will happen when you are hunting your dog later on real game.

Pigeons therefore are the trainer's answer, not only during initial training but also in the off season, when a little bird work by way of a refresher will help keep your dog fit and up to standard.

A small stock of pigeons, say ten or fifteen, can be quite easily kept. All that is required is a small roosting box secured to the end of a building with room for a corn tray and water pan. Birds kept in a roosting box for a couple of weeks will invariably fly right back to it when released or flushed, enabling you to use them repeatedly. (Not all birds by any means need be shot.) If a light metal swinging gate is incorporated, the birds will quickly learn to land on a wooden platform in front of it and push their way back in.

When planting birds in the field it is necessary to dizzy them slightly. Swing them 'round for just a few seconds before dropping them in the grass. Though they quickly recover they are inclined to stay put for a considerable length of time, unless you are training in the evening, when the roosting urge tends to make them fly off sooner.

It is essential for the flushing dog that the bird be awake and alert, ready to take flight the moment the dog bears down on it. Thus, the head should not be placed beneath the wing when the bird is planted, as this keeps the bird asleep (a method used only in the training of the pointing breeds).

In training the flushing dogs I prefer planting pigeons in the manner I have described, rather than using wire cages or traps from which the bird is released by a cord or electronic signal. Planting your birds by hand ensures a more natural flush. You are creating a situation as similar as possible to the real thing: a

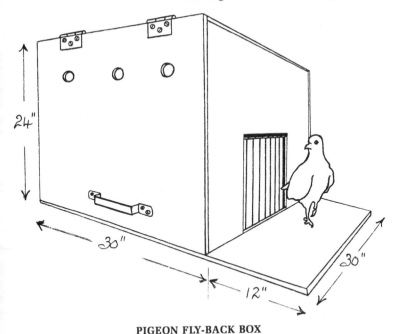

PIGEON FLY-BACK BOX

game bird being flushed in the wild. (The electronic device referred to above, which not only releases but actually propels the
bird into the air, can be put to good use for the pointing breeds,
especially when a dog is persistently not holding the point.
Enough birds released directly in front of the dog as he closes,
so that he doesn't trap any, will quickly teach him the futility of
dropping his point and going in.)

Try to avoid planting pigeons in cover too deep or too thick.
Under such conditions a pigeon is unable to become airborne
quickly enough, as it uses only its wings to lift off (unlike the
pheasant, which employs its legs by springing up). Cover too
dense results in too many birds being trapped, so choose slightly
more open patches for more successful flushes. Once planted, a
good flier will not normally make its way into thick cover. A bird
that has been wing-clipped however usually will, the instinct for
self preservation no doubt taking over.

When walking out to plant, remember that you are laying a

track or trail through the grass. A line of scent is created, primarily by your footwear, and a young gun dog may quickly learn to search for your line of scent and follow it to the bird. Since it is essential for any gun dog to learn to quarter, investigating all the cover ahead of him, he must be prevented from getting into the habit of trailing foot scent. It will help if you avoid walking up the center of the field while planting. Otherwise as your dog hunts he will be crisscrossing your line of scent all the way along. This is a sure way of spoiling a good quartering pattern. Try to walk in from the extreme sides of the area to be worked. Having dropped the first bird walk back out of the field along the same line and cut back in further along to plant the second bird . . . and so on (see diagram). You can then cast off your dog and hunt him with his chances of coming upon your scent trail considerably minimized.

SCENT TRAIL TRAINING

Most well-bred gun dogs have the inherent ability to follow a line of scent. This extremely valuable talent, though mainly hereditary, can and must be enhanced by training, as the situation to which it applies—trailing a wounded or running bird—is often encountered in the field.

Scent trail training requires the creation of a line of scent clearly separate from your own. To achieve this it is best to enlist an assistant. It can also be done working alone (employing a method I will describe in a moment), but first we will consider scent trail laying with someone helping.

When scent trail laying, leave your dog either in the car cage or in his kennel (if close by) so that he is out of sight of your activities. Dogs are smart, inquisitive creatures and love to watch what you are doing, especially if something connected with bird work is suspected. To allow the dog to watch you actually laying the scent track and dropping the dead bird at the end would make the exercise pointless. On being brought out and released the dog would likely as not head straight for the bird without putting his nose to the ground. Teaching the dog to use his nose and puzzle out for himself what route the bird has taken is the whole object of what I am about to describe.

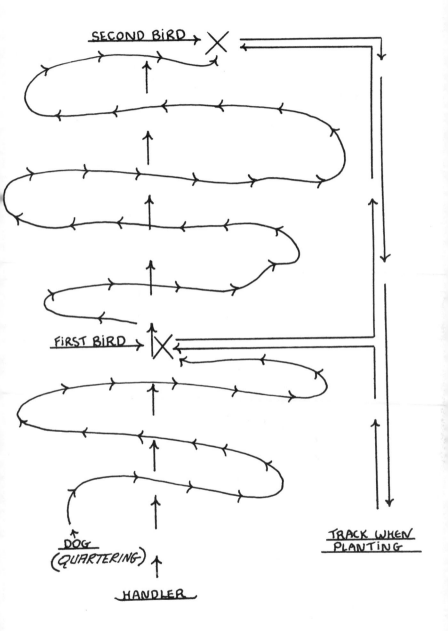

SECOND BIRD →

FIRST BIRD →

DOG
(QUARTERING)

HANDLER

TRACK WHEN
PLANTING

MINIMIZING SCENT TRAIL WHEN BIRD PLANTING

A trail of scent sufficient for a dog to follow can be made simply by dragging a retrieving dummy, but I see little point in doing this and much prefer to use a dead bird. You will need a length of light cord (two 30-foot check lines tied together are ideal). To the center of this line tie a piece of cord about two feet long, and to this cord firmly attach a dead pigeon, chukar partridge, or quail. In carrying out this exercise avoid days that are hot and dry and breezy, as scenting conditions are usually not good in such weather. Cloudy, cool, damp days are the best. Scent tends to lie well and is easy to follow. Remember, we are not trying to fool the dog. We are trying to train him.

Your assistant and yourself should each take an end of the rope, and keeping as far apart as possible from each other drag the carcass through the grass in a straight line for thirty or forty yards, leaving a second dead bird at the end of the trail. Allow a few minutes for the scent to settle, then go get your dog and cast him off to hunt at the start of the line. On finding the line he will in all probability waver from side to side, but do not interrupt him provided he is making some headway. Just keep quiet and allow him time to sort things out for himself, and be sure to give him lots of praise when he locates the bird (which should be retrieved to hand).

Change direction each time you lay a trail. As your dog's ability improves, increase the trail's length and put in turns to the left and right. Within a relatively short time, given the right ground and weather conditions, trails two-hundred to three-hundred yards in length should present no problem and you can start varying the find at the end by occasionally leaving a wing-clipped bird instead of a dead one.

As your dog becomes more proficient at trailing it will become necessary to use your stop whistle to "Hup" him if he is moving too fast for you to keep up. A dog trailing too fast and far ahead can often mean a missed shot opportunity if the bird flies.

If help is not available, attach the bird to the end of the line instead of to the middle. Then swing it around and around and cast it out as far as possible into the field. Make the throw from a path or track. Drag the bird slowly, as you walk along the track, taking care to keep the bird in the grass and not let it come out onto the track. When the bird reaches a point close to you, throw

Preparing to lay a scent trail. Two check lines are clipped together and a cord attached, to which a dead bird can be fastened.

Laying a scent trail using a dead pheasant. Note that the distance between the trail layers has been reduced to fit them into the photograph. In practice they should keep as far apart as the ropes allow.

a dead bird out onto the trail at least two or three yards from where you were walking. Then get your dog, walk 'round to your starting point, and cast him off. Obviously only shorter trails are possible doing it this way, but they are of equal value in teaching the rudiments of trailing.

Undoubtedly the best bird trailing springer I have ever owned is "Bracken," whom we brought over to the United States from England when he was a puppy of twelve weeks. I trained him here in the U.S. and he has in fact had a number of placings in field trials for me. He is of course steady to wing and shot, will take hand signals on land and water, and possesses the most uncanny marking ability in the toughest of cover conditions. I work him at one or two private club shoots and I always have the fullest confidence that sent out for a wing-tipped bird he will come up with it. His ability to follow a cripple over considerable distances is at times astonishing. Still in his prime and with a wonderful temperament he is a joy to own and hunt with.

6

Advanced Training For Upland Hunters

IT IS ESSENTIAL that any flushing dog be trained to keep within range when hunting. A flushing dog hunting beyond the range of your gun is out of control and of little use. Most spaniels and retrievers work close naturally, at least up to the time they start to get onto birds and scent. Then there may be a tendency, through excitement and over-enthusiasm, to range out further than advisable. It is therefore necessary that your dog be trained not only to keep within shooting distance but also to develop a pattern that will cover all the ground ahead of and to each side of you.

This pattern is known as *quartering*. (See diagram entitled *MINIMIZING SCENT TRAIL WHEN BIRD PLANTING* in previous chapter.)

The maximum range allowable for a quartering flushing dog is in my opinion 20 yards to the left and right and 10 yards out straight ahead. You should be aided here by your earlier practice, when exercising the dog as a pup, of not allowing him to get out of shooting range when running free.

It is well to start your dog quartering by hunting him into the wind. Cast him out by giving a wave of the arm to the left or right together with the command "Hie On." If he hunts in the required direction, keep walking straight ahead and as he reaches the maximum range of his cast whistle him to turn. The signal can be given one of three ways: (a) two pips on the whistle, (b) a mouth whistle—which having been decided on should always be given the same way and for one purpose and one purpose alone, or (c) the command "Come Round." Most dogs seem to react more readily and quickly to a whistle than they do to the human voice, but I recommend that if an artificial whistle is used the command "Come Round" be used in conjunction. This is because at times you may forget to take your whistle along with you, and furthermore there will be times, especially when hunting in bitterly cold weather, when to have to fiddle around for the whistle will be less than a blessing.

As your dog turns, wave him across with your other arm . . . and so on up the field. Most dogs take to this readily. For those who do not it may be necessary for you to alter your course to the left or right—away from the dog—in an effort to better his pattern. In other words, when you cast him off to the left, alter your direction slightly to the right without his noticing.

If a dog needs more incentive, it can help considerably to take along with you three or four dead pigeons (or even dummies) concealed in a pocket or bag. As your dog is hunting and as you move out and away from the direction in which he is at the time headed, throw one of the pigeons out ahead and well to the side of you so that on his next cast back he will pass downwind of the fall, locate the bird, and bring it back to you. This should be continued both to the left and right as you continue up the field. Be extra vigilant to ensure that the dog does not see you throwing the birds as he will start to watch you in anticipation instead of concentrating on hunting. This exercise not only helps a dog's pattern but also helps maintain his interest. A dog can go stale from too much "dry hunting" (hunting without reward).

If your dog does see you throwing the birds and as a result starts to watch your hands, discontinue the throwing method and instead plant the birds at staggered intervals up the field beforehand. Then bring the dog from his kennel and hunt him as

Teaching a spaniel to quarter. An even pattern should be maintained while the handler walks as straight a course as possible. Turning the dog within shooting distance is vital.

before. When putting the birds out remember to do it in such a way as to avoid the dog's starting to trail your scent.

It should not be long before your dog is quartering nicely ahead of you and turning smartly to your whistle or command. As he improves, gradually stop the whistle/command and arm signals. Resort to a command only if he fails to turn automatically at the end of a cast. Eventually you will find that commands and signals need hardly be used at all.

It is important to remember that wind direction will have a great effect on how your dog will hunt. If the wind is blowing from your left he will tend to work deeper to your right, and the opposite if the wind is blowing from the other direction. If you are working downwind (with the wind at your back), you will find a tendency for your dog to pull out ahead, turn into the wind, and hunt back toward you. Any experienced dog will use the wind to his best advantage.

It should also be noted that a consistent quartering pattern is not always possible in tough cover conditions and woodland. Under such circumstances you must go along with your dog and get yourself through as best you can. Hunting along hedgerows is another situation which has to be treated differently. Try always to walk on the downwind side of the hedgerow. In this way the bird scent within the row will be blown toward you, which means the dog will be hunting from your side and thus be that much more controllable.

Where nose work is concerned, always trust your dog. Don't ever think you know better than he, even if you did see the pheasant run into the edge of the corn at a certain point. Once your dog is in there after the bird, go along with him and don't try to show him what you presume he should do. A good friend of mine back in England gave me this piece of advice years ago and I have found it over and over again to be reliable. You will sometimes forget, and force your dog to hunt the way you think he should hunt, rather than the way he is hunting . . . and in nine cases out of ten you will be proven wrong.

FACING COVER

Now that the essentials of quartering have been taught, a further step and an important one in the education of any upland hunting dog must not be overlooked, and that is teaching him to hunt in thick cover conditions. So far the teaching has taken place mainly in open fields, where the fullest attention could be brought to bear on the dog's responses. It is now necessary to have him hunt in woodland and dense cover, in which a perfect quartering pattern is not possible. He must now learn to hunt out of sight of you, remembering still to remain within shooting distance.

Choose a location with three- or four-foot-high brush and scrub and take with you three or four dead pigeons. You will almost certainly find that in conditions such as this the dog's tendency will be to stay in much closer, which is good and should be encouraged. If he gets out too far—not necessarily due to disobedience—change your direction and give the whistle signal to turn him and get him back in toward you. Such tactics on your part will tend to make him more aware and careful.

Most spaniels have a great love of thrashing their way through thick cover, the tougher the going the better. They will force their way into the thickest of brush for the sheer love of it. This is not so with the retriever breeds however. Their love of cover is not nearly so strong unless they have marked a downed bird, in which case any retriever worth its salt will pitch in and root the bird out at once. Most, however, have a tendency to sidestep rough cover and hunt 'round the edges, plunging in only when the presence of game has been definitely detected.

If you are able to hunt your dog in an area where you are fairly sure game scent is present, so much the better. For the dog that lacks drive there's nothing like a few flushed pheasants to encourage more enthusiastic hunting. (The degree to which a dog is enjoying his work will show in his tail action.)

If game is scarce, use dead pigeons. Unobtrusively throw them into the cover to the left and right—and of course out of sight of the dog. Then work him in such a way that he will pass downwind of each bird. Each time he pushes in to make a retrieve encourage him by pointing to the cover and saying "Hie On."

Give him four or five finds each session, and if natural game is not present use live pigeons occasionally. It is very important that having pushed his way into the thicker places your dog should be rewarded with a retrieve or a flush from time to time. This will spur him on to keep plunging into the thicker cover, which when you are hunting afield is of course where the game is most likely to be.

DROPPING TO SHOT AND WHISTLE

The object here is to have your dog (a) sit steady on flushing a bird, (b) remain sitting when you shoot, (c) not move until commanded to retrieve, and (d) if the bird is missed, ignore the bird and resume hunting when commanded.

So far, sitting to whistle has been done only with your dog close alongside you at heel. Now we are going to expand on this. You will require your pupil to sit to whistle while in the course of hunting. For this you will require, in addition to your whistle, the blank pistol.

Start your dog off hunting and after two or three casts be ready for him to turn and head back toward you. As he does so, suddenly give a single blast on the whistle and raise your right arm (which should be holding the pistol) and simultaneously fire a shot. You may be surprised to find that your dog will stop and sit down perfectly, but rest assured that the cause of this will almost certainly be surprise on his part also. Don't take initial success to mean that you have won. Considerably more time will be required to ensure that your pupil will comply instantly whether coming toward you or going away. Remember too that you are not yet at the stage of throwing dummies or dead birds (which constitute an additional temptation), so regard any initial success with scepticism. Alternate the command "Hup" with the whistle signal. It is important to teach the dog to stop and sit on this command also, because in natural hunting conditions, when a bird is flushed the chances are you won't have time to use a whistle. The automatic reaction, at least for a while (until such time as he sits automatically), will be to give the command "Hup." You may well ask "Why bother with the whistle at all?" The answer is that you will want your dog to stop to whistle for advanced training in direction control and blind retrieves. Before any direction signals can be given a dog should be stationary

Teaching dropping to shot and whistle. The gun is raised as Bruiser, a springer spaniel, is hunting.

The shot is fired together with one blast on the whistle and the dog sits.

and watching you, and to achieve this at considerable distances your best bet is the whistle.

If there is any tendency on the dog's part to be slow about sitting, or to run on ahead for a few yards after the command has been given and the shot fired, take him back to where he was when you first signaled him. Shake him up a little and make him sit with a blast on the whistle and the command "Hup." A shot at this time is not necessary. Try to ensure that he reacts immediately. If he thoroughly absorbs what is required of him now, you will have little difficulty later, when birds are introduced into the scheme of things.

Let him remain sitting for several seconds before giving him the command to hunt on ("Hie On" plus a snap of the fingers). Do not be in a hurry to release him. Making him stay a moment helps reinforce in his mind that steadiness is required of him. While he is sitting, move around a little. Re-load if you wish. Don't get into the habit of standing still for fear that the slightest movement on your part will propel the dog into action. Be relaxed. He must realize that one thing and one thing only allows him to move, and that is your command to do so.

It is also a good practice to vary the direction in which you cast the dog off when he resumes hunting. (The reason for this will become apparent later in this chapter.)

When he will stop and sit promptly to your whistle, shot, and command, whether close to you or well away from you, and remain where he is until commanded to hunt on, you are both ready to progress. But before you do, be quite satisfied that he is steady. The temptation to run in when dummies and birds are thrown is enormous. Reliable steadiness must first be attained without their use, or it surely will never be gained with them.

STEADINESS TO DUMMIES AND DEAD BIRDS

The object in having an upland dog steady to flush and shot is to prevent him from running on too far in pursuit of a missed bird, thereby disturbing other game. Apart from the personal satisfaction derived from working a dog trained to this standard, when hunting in the company of others who appreciate a dog of this type your sense of fulfillment will be great.

Before starting on live bird work you want to make sure your dog—while hunting—will stop and "Hup" willingly when a dummy or dead bird is thrown.

Have with you your whistle, the blank pistol, and a dummy. Start your dog hunting and allow him a few minutes and several casts to settle down. Take from your pocket the dummy, and when he turns at the end of a cast and is hunting back in your direction again, give the command "Hup" (by whistle or by voice), fire a shot, and with your free hand throw the dummy. Having had this maneuver described to you you may think it would be a distinct advantage to be a contortionist to coordinate all this! Have faith though, and you will find that the thing can be done quite easily.

As you throw the dummy do not watch it. Do not look to see where it falls. The temptation to do so will be considerable, but instead watch your dog to make sure he stays. Also, throw the dummy so that it falls at a point leaving you directly between it and your dog. You are now positioned to intercept him should he decide to break. If you carried out your basic training thoroughly enough it is unlikely he will break. If he does, blast the whistle again and yell "Hup" loudly. Give him the raised arm signal to reinforce matters. Run to him, get hold of him, and take him back to where he was when you hupped him in the first place. Make him hup and then walk off yourself to gather the dummy while he watches. Start over again. The chances are good that this time he will comply, having received your sharp and sudden reminder. Pause for a few seconds. If he remains good and steady, command him to retrieve.

Remember you are to let him retrieve only some of the dummies, while walking out to collect the others yourself.

Now, if all goes well for four or five throws, you should stop training for the day. After several more sessions you may substitute a dead pigeon for the dummy, throwing the bird out in exactly the same way. You will find that your dog will immediately notice the difference. His interest will increase, so remain vigilant and be ready to act quickly to check any sign of movement. If the least unsteadiness is apparent do not hesitate to go back to the dummy again. As long as your dog is unsteady to dead birds it is pointless to start on live ones.

The pupil having learned to hup to whistle, the dummy is used—then dead birds, and finally live ones.

You should also at this point start getting your dog accustomed to the command "Gone away." This command indicates to him that a bird has been missed or to break him off a trail you do not want him to follow. Commence by saying "Gone away" each time you pick up the dummy or dead bird while he sits and watches. Say it also when he flushes a pigeon which you either miss or deliberately allow to fly off unscathed. The purpose of this command is to break his concentration, to divert his attention from the departing bird, which he must understand is not retrievable, and to bring him back onto your wavelength once more.

We will assume that all has gone well for several sessions with dead birds, and that you now feel your dog is ready for some live bird work. Before you start, sit down and mull over each stage of his training to date. Be sure he is reliably proficient at each stage. Set aside a morning or afternoon and take him through each phase once more. (1) Walk him to heel and sit him to command and whistle. (2) "Hup" him and go away, making sure he stays put until you return. (3) Make sure he is steady to thrown and fired dummies while he is sitting alongside you. (4) Dispatch him to retrieve a dummy. When he is halfway out, give him the whistle signal to "Hup" and make sure he does and stays put. Then send him on ahead for the bird. (5) Conclude with the thrown dummy and dead bird exercises while he is hunting.

If he performs satisfactorily, he is ready for live bird work.

STEADINESS TO LIVE BIRDS

My method of introducing a young upland hunting dog to live birds is to carry two or three pigeons in my game pocket and to release them one at a time—with a blank shot fired—while the dog is hunting. (This is done in exactly the same way as it was done during the dead bird exercise.) If he hups and remains steady each time you do this (and remember, the temptation to break is now at its greatest), the next time before you bring him out plant three birds in the field a hundred yards or so apart. Then go fetch your dog and hunt him upwind towards the birds. It will be best if you can have a friend along to do the shooting while you concentrate exclusively on the dog. If it is you doing the gunning your concentration will be off the dog at the very moment he is likeliest to break and run in. As he is hunting, try to maneuver yourself so that you are relatively close to the dog at the moment he flushes the first bird. The instant he flushes the bird you must give both the whistle and verbal command to "Hup." Watch your dog carefully. Ignore the line of flight of the bird and for the present do not concern yourself with where it falls. Your dog and partner will have it marked. I prefer that at least one bird be purposely allowed to fly off with a shot fired in the air, and also that the dog be allowed to retrieve only one bird. Remember to use the command "Gone away" when necessary, and cast the dog off in a direction opposite to that in which the bird has flown.

By doing this you are directing his mind away from the bird and focusing his attention on hunting again. Moreover, by casting him off *away* from the direction in which the bird flew away, you eliminate the possibility of his wrongly interpreting your arm signal and command as an order to retrieve.

If all has gone well, whether the birds have been shot or missed, stop training for the day and put your pupil back in his kennel. I

Once steadiness to thrown dummies and dead pigeons has been thoroughly learned, hunting up live, planted pigeons can be started.

A good hard flush by Bracken.

The dog hups (with a reminder on the whistle) as the bird flies off . . .

. . . and remains sitting while the handler shoots the bird.

After a suitable pause, the dog is sent for the bird . . .

. . . and successfully delivers to hand.

am a great believer in allowing a dog to think things over, not only the things that have gone well but also the problems that have been encountered and the corrective measures that have been taken. A little quiet meditation for a day or so can help work wonders the next time out.

If your dog breaks and runs in do exactly as advised before. Run to him, grab him, haul him back to where he was, sit him down, and reinforce matters by blowing the whistle and giving the "Hup" command. Repeating this in writing may well be boring. In training, repetition is the only way to success.

Wherever possible your friend, or you, should never shoot a bird when your dog has broken. If the dog breaks and the bird that caused him to break is subsequently shot, and the dog, having broken, cannot be stopped before getting his mouth on the downed bird, then attaining reliable steadiness becomes just that little bit more difficult. So have your friend or assistant understand that he must be ready, when a bird flushes, to hear you shout "No" and to let the bird fly on without a shot being fired. The sooner the dog realizes that retrieves, i.e. rewards, only follow steadiness, the more enjoyable his life—and yours—will be.

When the dog traps a bird before it can fly, that bird should be treated as a normal retrieve and be brought to hand unharmed. This will not interrupt the steadying process as the dog has not, prior to coming upon and catching the bird before it flew, been given any whistle or verbal command to "Hup." Field trial spaniels are not penalized for trapping birds, and in fact with certain types of dogs trapping birds occasionally increases the dog's drive and speed.

As steadiness has been enforced gently but firmly all the way through the training process, it should by now have become second nature to your dog to such an extent that the thought of running in before being commanded to do so is hardly likely to enter his head. And it is at this stage that you have probably come to realize just how important the basic routine training has been, and how valuable it was to achieve artificial steadiness before going on to the real thing. There is no shortcut to training if you intend from the start that your dog be brought through to the highest standards. Apart from having a good sound prospect to begin with, time and patience are the two factors you will find most important.

So you have now reached what probably seems to you the pinnacle of success. Quite likely you originally regarded as unattainable that which you have now achieved. All the hard work, patience, and at times aggravation now seem to have been worthwhile. But be wide awake. For a considerable time yet at all training sessions with live birds you must be vigilant to ensure that no slip-ups occur. If they do, it's your fault, not your dog's.

Now for the time being we will leave the upland hunting dog and concentrate on advanced training for the non-slip retriever.

7

Advanced Training For Non-Slip Retrievers

IN DISCUSSING THE first stages of teaching a dog to walk to heel I stated that it is essential, with any dog which is going to be used strictly as a non-slip retriever, that heel work be done not only on but off the leash as well. We will assume that this training has been done and that your dog will now walk to heel steadily and reliably at all times. (No dog should be walked in the vicinity of traffic without being leashed, no matter how reliable he is walking to heel elsewhere. The best and most experienced dogs can forget and the outcome can be heartbreaking. All that is needed is for a cat suddenly to run across your path or for another dog, wandering loose, to threaten your own, and you have all the elements for a chase and possible disaster. Always have your light nylon slip-cord leash in your pocket therefore, to use near traveled roads.)

As a means of testing your dog's steadiness while he is off the leash and walking to heel, have someone occasionally and unexpectedly throw a retrieving dummy or dead pigeon across your path with an accompanying shot from the blank pistol. When this happens command your dog to "Hup" either verbally or with the whistle. As the real object of this exercise is not retrieving practice, but rather the testing of steadiness at heel, don't send the dog out for every retrieve—maybe only one in six.

That most useful command "Gone away" should begin to be brought into play now. It should be given every time a bird is missed, or whenever it is your intention to leave the dog sitting while you or your assistant picks up instead. Continue using "Gone away" throughout training. As I stated previously it is a means by which you can indicate to your dog that a missed bird should be forgotten. If two young retrievers can be tested this way together, each with his owner, and the occasional retrieve being taken in rotating turn—the non-participating dog honoring the one retrieving by sitting at heel, so much the better. It will of course under these circumstances be necessary for a third person to be present to do the dummy and dead bird throwing.

Up until now all retrieving has been carried out with your dog sitting by your side while you threw or fired the dummies yourself. If under these new circumstances he shows any tendency to want to run in, check him immediately with the "No" command and get him back in to heel. If necessary have him trail the leash for a short time until he has got accustomed to things being done the way you want them done.

Leaving him sitting while you yourself walk out to collect the dummy or bird will remind him that not every retrieve can be his. Only your voice command can ever be regarded as being the signal to go.

STOPPING TO WHISTLE

Both the upland hunting dog and the retriever were started sitting to whistle during preliminary training, but this was taught only while the dog was walking along at heel. We must now progress to teaching the retriever to respond to the stop whistle from a distance, and it is now that the value of the earlier start on this will become apparent.

You want to teach the retriever to stop to whistle so that (a) the dog can be brought under control, (b) he is better able to concentrate on you for further orders, and (c) he can be more easily directed to the fall of a bird which he has not seen. For a re-

Heel work off the leash with a non-slip retriever.

The dummy is thrown, the shot fired, and the dog commanded to hup. This is excellent steadiness training.

Steadiness should be enforced by having the dog sit and stay while dummies are thrown both right . . .

. . . and left . . .

. . . and picked up by the handler . . .

. . . as the dog looks on.

A good test . . .

. . . and will teach your dog manners.

triever to be able to do this well is invaluable, particularly when duck hunting. Imagine circumstances whereby you have just sent your dog off for a retrieve that he was able to mark, but all of a sudden while he is away a second duck flights in, presenting itself nicely for a shot. What are you going to do? Decline the shot because your dog is out of sight and will therefore be unable to mark the bird if it falls across the creek? Shoot the bird and swim for it yourself?

If your dog has been taught to stop to whistle and take hand signals, you have no problem.

Hand signal training will come later, but the first step toward that goal we will deal with now.

Having first ordered your dog to "Hup," walk away from him twenty yards or so and then, after pausing for a few seconds, call him to you verbally and by giving the recall whistle (several pips). To keep him guessing, vary slightly the length of time you wait before calling him. After doing this several times, choose an opportune moment and as he is returning—and is about halfway back to you, suddenly give one blast on the whistle and raise your right hand high. This will no doubt surprise him, as it did the upland dog, and he will either sit right down or keep coming a few more faltering steps, head lowered, trying to figure out what on earth you are doing now.

Walk out towards him, take him back to the spot where he was when you tried to stop him, and repeat the signals so that he sits. Say "Good dog" and walk away again, leaving him there. Repeat the exercise, and this time, likely as not he will comply, though perhaps rather slowly. If he does comply, praise him from where you are standing and then walk a little further away and give it another try. If your initial training was thorough enough he will quickly grasp, after several sessions over a period of a week or two, what is required of him. Eventually you will be able to stop him at considerable distances, and do it two or three times as he is approaching you.

You may notice, for a while at least, a tendency for him to come in slowly, anticipating the stop whistle each time. So vary matters by occasionally allowing him to run all the way in to you without stopping him enroute. This should make sure that his return to you remains fast.

Dogs vary tremendously in their reaction to this exercise. Some take to it easily, with little or no hesitation. Others regard being suddenly stopped and made to sit as a punishment for something they have done wrong. The latter type of dog will react slowly and with hesitation, but with gentle handling and patience—and if necessary an occasional retrieve by way of a reward—you should soon be able to teach him that he is not being stopped as a punishment, but rather so that he can receive a further command to locate and bring his favorite prize, the dummy or a bird.

Once you feel your dog is doing this exercise consistently well, you can begin throwing the dummy and after sending him to retrieve, stopping him with the whistle when he is halfway there. Then, provided he has complied, send him on. Any problems encountered should be treated in precisely the same way as before, by taking hold of him and putting him back where he was and trying again.

Some handlers are satisfied if their dog simply stops and stands still before being redirected, but I prefer, and strongly recommend, that the dog be required to sit also. This way you not only have better control but will get better attention when you start to teach hand signals.

STEADINESS TO BIRDS ON LAND AND WATER

Unlike the upland dog, who has to be trained to be steady to the birds it flushes while hunting, the non-slip retriever normally spends most of his time sitting close by his master in a blind or a boat waiting for duck to flight. That the retriever is already immobile, and was commanded to *hup* long before the birds' arrival, tends to make steadiness training somewhat easier.

As you are presumably satisfied that your dog is thoroughly reliable in all that has been taught so far (a test similar to that advised for the upland dog will be time well spent), you can now advance to training for steadiness to live birds. Have a friend go along with you with a crate of eight or ten live pigeons and his shotgun. Have him set up 30 to 40 yards away while you sit your dog at heel. The birds should be released one at a time. Have a shot fired as each bird flies, and try to see to it that one or two birds are actually killed for the dog to retrieve. Remember to give the command "Gone away" each time a bird is either accidentally or deliberately missed, making certain that the dog's attention is diverted from the departing bird to yourself.

Each time a bird is down, be extra vigilant in checking your dog for any sign of intention to break. Should you become concerned that this may happen, clip on the check line and stand on it. But only resort to this if absolutely necessary.

Before sending him to retrieve, pause for a while. Then, by giving the hand signal in front of his head accompanied by the verbal command "Fetch," send him. If he is marking well from this range, extend the distance between yourself and your partner by ten yards or so. Continue this until your pupil is coping consistently well at ranges of sixty to eighty yards. Check firmly any tendency toward overanxiousness, using the word "No." Live birds create in any dog the greatest excitement and enthusiasm of all. Make him wait longer if necessary, never allowing a retrieve if he moves forward by so much as a couple of feet before being commanded.

It is now important that you be using the shotgun as well as, or even instead of, the blank pistol, as the difference in sound is considerable and dogs react quite differently to the real thing as compared to the artificial.

Do not confine yourself to having all the birds flown from some distance away. Vary matters by having your partner stand alongside you and the dog, as temptation increases when the birds are closer. In shooting ducks the gun will be fired from a position quite close to the dog anyway, so you had better start getting him accustomed to this.

The next step, as with the upland hunting dog, is to walk out into the field (before taking the dog out) and at intervals of 100 yards plant three or four pigeons or maybe chukars. Afterwards bring out the dog and walk him to heel and off the leash upwind towards the birds so that each is flushed in turn as you approach. Strong pigeons planted lightly will get up more than willingly when you get too close. As they fly off have your dog *hup* at heel and fire a shot in the air, keeping him sitting there a few seconds before walking on. Remember to keep an eye on him as you raise your gun to shoot. This is the very time that your attention is diverted from him, and he knows it, so be ready to act quickly and firmly if he moves. This can be a useful form of training for a retriever. Imagine walking to your duck blind one dark winter morning, with your dog at heel, when suddenly a roosting pheasant erupts at your feet. The exercise described above will help ensure that your dog will not take off after the bird and spend the next fifteen minutes careening round the marsh disturbing every duck that might already be there while you stand blasting on your whistle and cursing.

Also, during this exercise, try to down one of the birds—not necessarily the last—to reward your pupil with a retrieve.

Now it's time to go to a lake. Try to arrange things so you have a partner positioned to flight birds right out across the water. For some reason pigeons prefer not to fly over water if they can avoid it, and will turn as soon as possible. But by careful and thoughtful positioning you should be able to get at least one or two birds shot over the water. Quite frankly I am not very concerned about whether the birds you use are flyers or not. Where water work is concerned it is of little matter. Dead birds and dummies and the launcher can be used to just as good if not better effect as you are able to be more accurate.

A few flyers at first though can be a useful addition to the overall development of steadiness.

Most trainers, when working retrievers on advanced water work, introduce the dog to live birds by using "shackled" ducks. Obtaining ducks may present a problem for the amateur trainer though, so I suggest asking a professional if you may try the dog in his company. Most trainers will help if approached properly, and the experience the dog will gain will be most useful.

You have already done some retrieving work over a creek with dummies and dead birds, so practice can now be given with a few fliers in the same way, preferably with your partner again stationed on the far side of the water. No problem should be encountered if the exercises already outlined have gone well— marking being the all-important factor once more.

If your dog has been doing consistently well so far, he is ready for you to hunt. But bear in mind—as I pointed out for the upland hunting dog earlier—that a world of difference exists between the artificially presented bird and the wild one.

8

First Hunting Trips

WITH YOUR DOG steady to flush-and-shot on planted birds, you are ready to start hunting him on wild birds or at a shooting preserve.

Be prepared to discover that handling a dog under hunting conditions will be noticeably different from working him under training conditions, the main difference being that when training you know where—or approximately where—the birds are. You have the advantage of being able to anticipate, and thus to move into such a position in relation to your dog that when the bird is flushed you will be able to exercise better control. In wild bird hunting the unexpected happens constantly, and it is this element of surprise that makes concentration on your dog so much more important.

I recommend therefore that for the first two or three hunting trips you should confine yourself to handling the dog while you allow a friend to do the shooting. This way you will be in a far better position to ensure that what you have so painstakingly taught your dog in training will be remembered in the exciting and often giddy process of actual hunting. Sacrificing the pleasure of shooting for the first two or three trips will be well worth it in the long run, believe me.

A visit to a shooting preserve is an ideal way to expose your dog to a greater concentration of birds. Further, it is possible to start hunting on preserves relatively early in the fall, which will give your dog added valuable experience before the later-opening pheasant and grouse season.

When hunting, be mindful of all you have insisted upon so far. Keep your mind concentrated on your dog, especially when he is "making game" and a bird is flushed. You should by now be able to read his mind and know if he is even *thinking* about stepping out of line. Do not concern yourself with the direction of the fall when a bird is shot but be sure, after the dog has hupped, that he remains sitting for a suitable period of time before you send him to retrieve. If he moves forward so much as a few feet before being commanded to go, put him back where he was, and if possible pick up the bird yourself or ask your partner to get it. A yard or so of transgression the first time may become two or three the next. Nip any and all misbehavior in the bud straightaway.

Now there will be times when your dog will flush a bird from thick undergrowth and have to move out of the cover himself to watch the line of flight—which he would otherwise have been unable to see—and mark the fall. Obviously you must allow for such exceptions . . . but do insist on steadiness whenever he is in the clear. A good dog will quickly learn that he is allowed some leeway in thick cover, but must remain perfectly steady once in the open.

If any transgressions occur do not hesitate to correct the dog immediately, and if you think it necessary reimpress him with a short training session the next day. All the really hard work has now been done, and it would be pointless now to allow matters to deteriorate.

If a wounded bird falls in the open and takes off running in full view of the dog, do not send him for it while it is still in sight. Wait until it has disappeared from view before dispatching the dog. Sending him for the bird while he can still see it running is comparable to allowing him to chase a flier. Don't submit him to temptation. And be sure to follow him while he is trailing. If you

First hunting trips for pheasant. Having someone else along to gun so you can concentrate on the dog is advisable for the first few trips.

With one bird already in the bag, Bracken hunts out some typical pheasant cover . . .

A cock is flushed . . .

. . . rocketing straight up and away . . .

Bracken hups, his full attention on the bird and his handler's full attention on him!

The pheasant is hit . . .

. . . and the fall marked by the dog.

A nice soft-mouthed retrieve. Note that the gun is open—for safety.

The bird is correctly handed over.

see him locate the bird, whistle him to retrieve immediately, so that he will have the sense of doing it at your command and not on his own.

The same advice applies to a bird lightly pricked by shot. It is often quite difficult to be sure whether such a bird has been hit sufficiently hard, and it is far better, instead of sending the dog, gradually to hunt 'round toward where you last saw the bird, in the hope that the dog either locates and traps it or flushes it again. At least if it is flushed now you are close enough to exercise control and to take the opportunity for a second shot. To have sent him on a long and possibly futile retrieve could have resulted in a chase.

If you feel confident after two or three trips with your partner, start carrying the gun and doing the shooting yourself, preferably on your own. In the early days do not be tempted to want to shoot too many birds over the dog. Three or four in a couple of hours of hunting is plenty. Too many flushes and too much shooting can result in overexcitement and a temptation to riot, especially in a dog's first season.

A happy spaniel after a nice morning's hunt.

NON-SLIP RETRIEVERS

The same principles as apply to the upland hunting dog apply in general to the non-slip retriever. In other words, concentrating on maintaining the dog's steadiness should be uppermost in the handler's mind. With a retriever though it should not be necessary for a friend to go along with you to do the shooting. The retriever, sitting beside you, should be relatively easy to handle and control.

Having set up in your chosen spot, try to position your dog so that he has good uninterrupted view of things. When ducks come circling into view a quiet reminder to "Hup" is always advisable before you take a shot. After your shot the dog's concentration should be on the falling bird, so look back at the dog immediately and remember to wait before giving the order to retrieve. Do not under any circumstances be tempted to send the dog just as the bird hits the water, even if you know it's a cripple. Any lightly hit duck that has alighted on the water should be given a second barrel before you send the dog. It can be extremely difficult for a dog to catch a bird that is repeatedly diving, so rather than tire the dog and harrass the bird, it is far more humane to shoot again. The same applies to geese. Whether on land or water a wounded honker can be an extremely aggressive and formidable retrieve for a first-year dog.

If a bird is down and dead in the water it can be useful to leave it there—provided it is in no danger of being swept away—while you wait for a second to come in. In doing this you are reinforcing your dog's steadiness by reminding him that he must not assume that every bird is to be retrieved at once. If no further shot opportunities are forthcoming, within a reasonable length of time and while his mind is still on the original downed bird you may send him. The main thing is that you will have got the message home. In the same way dove hunting is also excellent control training, as often several birds will be dropped before a retrieve is permitted.

To maintain the standard your dog has attained, discipline yourself to accept occasional misses and missed opportunities. Be a dog man first and a hunter second and rest assured, you will be repaid.

Bess, a flatcoated retriever sits at a stand on an English pheasant shoot, her owner waiting for the birds to appear at the first drive.

A pheasant retrieved and handed over perfectly by Bess at a shoot in Wales. The flatcoated retriever is increasing in popularity again slowly but surely.

WOODPIGEON SHOOTING

One of the most exciting types of shooting, comparable to that of doves in this country, is woodpigeon shooting in Britain.

Woodpigeons are a totally wild strain of pigeon about the size of a racing or homing pigeon. They flight and feed in large flocks and roost in the highest branches in woodland at night. They provide firstclass sport requiring fast reaction and good marksmanship and shooting is normally carried out in one of two ways.

One method involves the use of "pigeon decoys" which are spread out on feeding areas after the flight lines to and from that area have been carefully reconnoitered and noted. The gunner, who has to be well camouflaged, retires to a hide or blind usually set up in a hedge or in bales of straw if on a large wheat or oat stubble field. "Woodies" are extremely wary and crafty, and the slightest movement on the part of the gunner is guaranteed to send the birds swinging away. Most pigeon shooters take along their labrador or spaniel to do the retrieving as it is unwise to leave dead birds scattered about the "decoy spread" because they simply alarm others flighting in.

Some dead birds are however "set up" by the use of small sticks as though they were feeding along with the decoys. And many birds can be shot this way by an experienced gunner in the course of a few hours. (As with all hunting in Britain there is no limit to the number of birds which may be taken.)

My own preference is for the second method, which is to wait in the winter woods for a couple of hours before dusk for the birds to come flighting in to roost.

It makes for sport hard to equal.

A wintry late afternoon in an oak and beech wood with the sun setting through the swaying, leafless treetops . . . suddenly a hundred pigeons, appearing as if from nowhere, slicing in against the gale with folded wings . . . the shooting fast and furious, snap shots taken through the branches of the trees as the birds jink and break away in every direction at the sound of the first shot. . . .

To have with you a young spaniel or retriever whose basic training has been finished is ideal, as several birds may be brought down among the trees and bramble bushes before the business of retrieving is gotten down to.

For enforcing steadiness and improving marking ability, experience of this sort is invaluable—and the birds make excellent eating in a casserole.

More's the pity we don't have woodpigeons here in the United States.

WORKING DOGS AT A HUNTING CLUB

An interesting and enjoyable aspect of gun-dog work—probably unthought-of by most dog enthusiasts—is that of working a gun dog for other sportsmen at a hunting club. The experience gained by both the dog and the handler is considerable, as more bird work is possible than when you are hunting for wild birds only. In addition, the opportunity is presented for enormously improving your dog's standard of training.

There are many preserves of the private type which would welcome a good handler and dog to help out. Often payment is made for your services, but even if this isn't forthcoming, the opportunity to work your dog where there is an abundance of birds can be reward enough in itself. If approached properly, the manager of a private shoot may well be interested in your going along on a regular basis, provided of course that you can satisfy him that you have a reliable and steady dog.

The shooting at these clubs usually takes two forms. First, normally in the morning, comes a tower release of pheasant or mallard, somewhat in imitation of a driven shoot, such as is common in Britain.

During the tower shoot birds are released from a high wooden platform, or, in some cases, just high ground, often concealed by trees. The guns, having drawn for their places, are positioned at numbered stakes situated at strategic points in a circle or semi-circle at some distance from the release point. Advantage is taken of the terrain in an effort to get the birds to fly as high as possible, although this is not always successful for the simple reason that birds that don't know where they're going never fly half so well as those that do. Every ten birds or so the guns change stands by moving up one, and so on. Releases of 150 to 300 birds are not uncommon.

It is the job of the handlers to be positioned well behind the circle of guns so that they and their dogs can mark the birds that have been shot, especially the wounded ones, and recover them as quickly and unobtrusively as possible. A dog should never be sent in front of the guns while a release is in progress. Only when the signal has been given for the guns to change stands should a retrieve be ordered. Birds *behind* the line can be collected immediately. An efficient Captain of Guns will have instructed everyone beforehand on the safety rules: no low shooting in front, behind, or to the side; no shots between releases.

It will be appreciated by any enthusiastic dog-handler that invaluable experience can be gained by picking up birds this way. You are able to locate your dog so that he can see bird after bird flying toward him as well as to the side. Some birds are shot. Others fly on, some even landing and running off into cover relatively close by. These are tempting conditions indeed, even for the most experienced of dogs. And too there will be a temptation on your part, when an obviously crippled bird lands, to send the dog immediately. But bear in mind my previous words of warning. Wait just that few seconds until the bird is out of sight. And use common sense, particularly in the first season, by not sending your dog on too long a retrieve, especially while shooting is taking place. If possible wait until the changeover. And walk a little closer to the point of the fall before sending your dog, as to send him sooner might result in his spotting a second bird (a flier) and becoming distracted and running in.

Spaniels as well as retrievers can be used for picking up on the tower shoot as the training you have done with both types should ensure that they will sit good and steady. I use springers most of the time for this, as I invariably did when picking up on driven pheasant shoots in England.

I want now to outline the system of "driven bird shooting" as practiced in the U.K., on which, as I have already said, the principles of the tower release are based.

Driven pheasant shooting has been a traditional part of the sporting scene in Britain since the latter end of the last century, the idea, it is said, having originated in Norfolk, which is in the eastern part of England in what is probably the finest wild pheasant area in the country.

There can be no doubt that the abundance of game in Britain is largely (if not solely) due to the number of private estates which have for generations employed gamekeepers to raise substantial numbers of pheasants and to a lesser extent, partridge.

Adult pheasants, trapped at the end of the shooting season, are held in a large stock pen. From April on the eggs are collected daily and hatched in incubators. The chicks are then turned out in batches in heated rearing units on the rearing field until about seven weeks of age, at which time they are taken to various parts of the estate and released into large pens before (after a relatively short stay) being allowed to wander out of the pens and become wild. To hold the birds on the estate feed is scattered by the Keepers each day along the woodland paths. But the birds are, by virtue of being free, gradually beginning to wander further out into the estate and more importantly becoming able to fend for themselves against predators.

By the time shooting commences in November the birds know the estate and its woods well and are totally wild and provide high, fast, sporting shooting. Driven days usually start with eight guns drawing for places—in other words points (or pegs)—where they will stand for the first drive.

After each drive they rotate places according to the custom of each individual shoot. The birds are put to flight (driven) by a party of anything from ten to twenty beaters, who are accompanied and supervised by the gamekeeper as they walk the woods slowly in line in order to flush the birds steadily towards and over the guns.

This type of shooting, far from being as easy as it may look to the bystander, is extremely challenging, as advantage is always taken of the lie of the land in order to have the birds flying as high and in as sporting a way as possible.

On most shoots five or six drives are the order of the day, with a break for lunch. No walk-ups take place afterwards as such estates stick rigidly to driven shooting.

Several dog handlers are present at every shoot—usually the same team season after season—and it is their job to pick up those shot birds, particularly the wounded runners, that are not

A tower shoot in Connecticut. A good high pheasant crosses the guns.

Returning at speed, General, a yellow lab, retrieves a pheasant from dense cover.

A typical release tower, set in the woods. Flag, for safety, denoting release in progress.

Picking up at the end of a tower shoot in Connecticut. The author working two yellow labradors, Sandringham General and Sandringham Gleam, who are brother and sister—both from England. (These birds were cripples, and without the dogs would not have been recovered.)

The end of an enjoyable morning's shoot in the late fall.

The results of a tower shoot in New York State.

A driven pheasant shoot in England. Some of the guns lined up below a wood that is being worked by the beaters. Here the pheasants fly out high, fast, and almost out of range.

An English cocker spaniel, Migdale Ben of Weavervale, retrieving a hen pheasant on a snowy day in England, where interest in cockers has revived considerably.

DRIVEN PHEASANT SHOOT—ENGLAND

lying out in the open field for the guns' own spaniels and retrievers to deal with.

The handlers' job is a vital one, not only helping to fill the game bag but in addition ensuring that as many pricked birds as possible are found and dispatched instead of being left to die.

Many of the large, privately owned estates have succumbed to crippling taxation and other modern-day financial strains, yet on most of them the shooting is maintained, if not on a private-ownership basis then by syndicates, which consist of say eight or ten guns who join together to pay for the shooting and the employment of the gamekeeper.

I cannot resist mentioning too the driven grouse shoots of Scotland, northern England, and Wales.

The red grouse of the open moorland are extremely hardy and thrive on the windswept heather-clad hills and mountains. Red grouse are strictly wild, none being artificially raised, and their numbers are being preserved, as with the pheasant, largely due to the existence of estates and gamekeepers. Not only is vigilant predator control practiced, but there is limited heather burning each spring to ensure a good growth of young heather shoots for feed.

. . . but back now to the club shoot here in the U.S.

In the afternoon, after lunch, your spaniel (or retriever, provided you trained him as an upland hunting dog too) can be used on the walk-up.

The walk-up involves a couple of hours' work with the dog and his handler accompanying a party of two or three guns. The object is to hunt up the birds missed during the morning's release. Here again is a golden opportunity to concentrate one-hundred percent on your dog while others do the shooting. The personal satisfaction derived from hunting a close-working, steady dog for people who usually only see hard-headed, out-of-control reprobates (their own dogs usually coming within this category) is quite rewarding. A surprising number of experienced guns are amazed to see a dog that is truly steady to flush and shot. The number of times that people have commented to me that they didn't realize that such a standard can be achieved is unbelievable. I find that most shooters are concerned with their own marksmanship (or lack of it) to the exclusion of all else. I sometimes ask all in the group with me, after the dog has flushed and then waited to be sent for the retrieve, if anyone can tell me what the dog did once the bird was in the air. Rarely can anyone do so, as all are usually too concerned with checking on who fired, how many times, and who connected! These are people who would never make dog handlers, no matter how hard they tried.

You can have a lot of fun and get a lot of good dog work done at the clubs, so why not ask around? Locate one or two local hunting clubs and go along and introduce yourself and your dog. You'll be glad you did.

9

Advanced Training–
Second Year

AT THIS POINT I will resume speaking simultaneously of the upland hunting dog and the retriever, though in the main the most frequent opportunities for double retrieves and the use of direction signals will be afforded the hunter who uses his dog strictly as a non-slip retriever for wildfowling.

A very sound practice, and one that should be borne in mind when conducting any form of retrieving exercise, is never to fool your dog. You should cultivate in him a trust so complete that he will know beyond any doubt that if you indicate to him that a retrieve is out there somewhere, then it darn well is. An awareness on his part that your word can be depended upon at all times is an asset worth its weight in gold, especially if direction control of any kind is to be successfully accomplished.

What comes next can be described as the icing on the cake, that little bit extra which, once learned, makes for a highly polished and finished hunting companion.

THE DOUBLE RETRIEVE

To start your dog on doubles have him sit alongside you. Use a pair of hand-thrown dummies or, if you prefer, two dead pigeons. Command the dog to *hup* and then throw both objects, one at a time, to your left and right. If necessary walk a few yards to increase the distance between falls, and be certain each time you throw that you have your dog's full attention. Do be sure that the dummies, or birds, are spaced well apart, almost at a forty-five-degree angle in fact, as this will avoid such confusion as might occur in the dog's mind if the falls were relatively close together.

Having thrown both objects, pause for a few seconds then send your dog in for the last one you threw. After taking delivery of it, turn and face in the direction of the second and sit your dog once more to sharpen his concentration.

Indicate the direction of the second fall with the usual hand signal and send him. He may, if you are lucky, remember the fall's location and go straight to it, or at least in its general direction. So long as he is making at least some effort in the area of the fall, leave him alone and keep quiet. If on the other hand he hesitates, puzzled, try to encourage him by repeating the command "Fetch" while walking along behind him, and when he locates the fall make much of him. Then walk back to the same spot as before, and repeat the exercise.

You may have to help him again and even a third time, but have patience. After only a few sessions of this your dog should start to remember that second fall regularly, and by continuing to use the same location (for the time being at least) and sending him always for the second dummy first, you will help him to succeed. In time, after handing the first retrieve over he will turn and sit down on his own, looking in the direction of the second, waiting anxiously for you to send him again.

Try to maintain this pattern until he is carrying it out consistently. Then, when you feel he has thoroughly grasped the idea, switch to sending him for the first retrieve first. Before sending him, turn him 'round and face him toward the object you wish him to fetch first. Give him the hand signal along with the command. Don't be surprised if he turns while running out and heads in the wrong direction. Be ready with the stop whistle and

Double retrieves: a dummy is thrown out to the left . . .

. . . then one to the right.

Amy is sent for the lefthand dummy first . . .

. . . then the righthand one.

The sequence should be reversed once the dog is starting to remember the second dummy.

bring him back and redirect him from his original position. Allowed time, any dog which has progressed well up to this stage will quickly grasp what you want of him. You should soon be able to send him quite confidently, in either order.

Once he is doing well with thrown dummies, the dummy launcher can be brought into service and used to add distance to the retrieves. Remember to fire the dummies at the same wide angle, using the wind to the dog's advantage if you can. For the time being at least, doubles at this distance should be in a field where the cover allows them to be easily marked, as we want the pupil to find the first one relatively quickly, giving him as little time as possible to forget the second. If he badly mismarks, stop him with the whistle. Gain his attention and use hand signals to get him back into the general area of the fall. It will be by watching your hands as well as having confidence in your commands that your dog will find it easier to assimilate the direction control training which comes next.

When he is marking and retrieving doubles well out on the field, try some on—and also across—the water. Take him to the creek and using precisely the same methods as on land, throw each dummy or pigeon onto the opposite bank, again well apart. As he has already done singles across the water—plus of course successful doubles on land, little difficulty should now be encountered other than occasional indecision about going for the second dummy. If the dog *does* hesitate, push him on out by hand signal and verbal command exactly as you would on land. A few successful finds over a relatively short period of time will increase his confidence.

Doubles on water can present certain difficulties, the primary problem being how to insure that both dummies stay in the area where they were thrown. You will find that the slightest wind or current will have moved the second dummy well away by the time the first has been retrieved, so try to choose a place where a fallen tree or some other obstruction will tend to hold the second dummy in place. In the case of the dummy to be retrieved first there is of course no problem, but with the second dummy it is essential, at least until your dog thoroughly understands direction signals, that the dummy stay where it landed.

DIRECTION SIGNALS

The basics of double retrieves have now been taught, but so far only from a position close at heel. The next stage involves doubles retrieved with the trainer using arm signals to direct the dog from a distance. I think this is an exercise well worth teaching any gun dog.

To start, take your pupil out into the field and tell him to *hup.* Walk away from him (no more than six or eight yards to begin with) and turn and face him. Have with you the usual two hand-thrown dummies or dead pigeons. Throw one well out to the side of the dog, at as near as possible to right angles to where he is sitting. Then throw the second well out—in precisely the opposite direction. Pause for a few seconds. Then, giving a clear signal by putting your arm straight out at shoulder level, give the command "Get out" and send him, preferably for the last one you threw. Always give the signal by using the arm corresponding to the direction in which you desire the dog to go. Don't get into the habit of using one arm for both directions, as the arm

Directional signals: Bracken is commanded to hup out in the field. One dummy is thrown to his left . . .

. . . another to his right.

This time Bracken is sent for the left dummy first.

He retrieves.

Having been put back where he was originally sitting, he is sent for the right-hand dummy . . .

. . . and retrieves again.

Teaching a dog to "Go back." The handler walks forward and throws the dummy beyond where the dog is sitting . . .

. . . then returns to his position, pauses, and gives a clear "Forward" arm signal together with the verbal command "Back." The dog starts to turn and move out towards the dummy behind him.

Returning in style!

can be seen less clearly at a distance when across the body. Given the signal, your dog will in all probability take off immediately and get the dummy without trouble. After he hands it over take him back to where he was sitting originally, walk back to where you were standing, and signal him to retrieve in the opposite direction.

At this juncture, as with the start of doubles from alongside you, he may have forgotten the second object, or may run in towards you rather than out to the fall. Have patience and persist in trying to get him out there. Walk sideways for a few yards in the direction of the fall, at the same time keeping your arm extended and repeating the command. Try to guide him on to the dummy in this way and when he succeeds, praise him well. It is again necessary to stick to the same retrieval order for some time. The dog must clearly understand what is required of him, and again you can help by taking advantage of the wind: *hup* him in such a position that the wind is blowing opposite to the direction in which the second object will be thrown. Then, if he fails to take a direct line immediately, he will get the scent more easily.

Gradually increase the distance at which you stand to give the signals. This should be done only a few yards at a time, the dummies being thrown out *before* you walk back to take up your position. Eventually you should be able to give your directions from thirty or more yards away and vary the order of the retrieves as much as you wish.

In time a third dummy can be introduced. This one should be thrown out beyond where the dog is sitting so that he can be sent straight out away from you. The hand signal to be used for this is the right arm raised high above the head. Then, with the command "Back," the arm should be waved forward to indicate to the dog that he must turn and head straight away from you. It is as well to start doing some of this now, before embarking on blind retrieves, as this is the signal you will be using for blind retrieve work.

Do not be tempted to rush things. Ensure that each stage is thoroughly understood and mastered before proceeding to the next.

BLIND RETRIEVES

The term "blind retrieve" simply means the retrieval by a dog of a dummy or bird which he has not seen fall. Many instances occur under normal hunting conditions—primarily with retrievers, while duck hunting—of a bird being shot out of sight of the dog. It might be that a bird is downed by a colleague who has no dog with him, or, if he has, whose dog is unable to locate it. In such a situation it can be a source of considerable pride to be the owner of a dog who can be sent out to locate and bring back a bird the location of which it does not know.

Much has been done already that will aid in teaching your dog blind retrieves. The hand signals already learned will be of the greatest value together with the command "Back," which was used to send the dog directly away from you for the third marked dummy.

I have employed several different methods over the years in the course of teaching spaniels and retrievers the blind retrieve. As is true with so many other aspects of training, some dogs react better to one particular way than to another. In general

Working two dogs together. When thoroughly steady—and not before—two dogs can be given retrieving practice simultaneously.

Bracken and Gleam are put through their paces with the dummy launcher . . .

. . . Bracken honoring first.

though I have found that the method I am about to describe is the one that most dogs seem to grasp, and it is the one I find myself resorting to now almost to the exclusion of any other.

First hup your dog, then walk out in a straight line for about thirty yards and let him see you drop a dummy or pigeon. Choose an area where the grass is several inches deep. Walk back to the dog and past him for two or three yards, then turn, pause, and give the arm signal and the command "Back." He will almost certainly retrieve, as he saw you drop the object. Repeat this a few more times, walking out to the same spot to drop the dummy. After several successful retrieves this way, walk out and change your tactics by dropping the dummy unobtrusively, so that he doesn't realize you've done so, then walk back and send him again. He may well have no problem again. More likely, however, because he did not see you drop the dummy he will run out so far, get confused, and start to mill around. If he does this stop him immediately with the stop whistle, and having gained his attention give him the "Back" command and hand signal again. If he hesitates, walk forward repeating the verbal command and signal and push him on toward the fall. Praise him as soon as he finds it and repeat twice more in exactly the same manner. He will almost certainly begin to understand and go straight to the fall.

Leave the exercise for the day after a good find.

Next day, take him out again to the same location but this time take two dummies with you. Command him to hup and walk out along the same line as before, but this time go ten yards further and without his seeing you do it, drop the first dummy. Walk back toward him again and at about the same point that the retrieves were being done from the day before, drop the second dummy. Having again walked a few yards past him, send him for the dummy closer to you, remembering to use the stop whistle and push him on if necessary, and also to praise him when he's successful. Send him for the furthest dummy the same way, and be prepared for him to go only as far as the point where the first dummy was placed. As he hunts there, use your stop whistle again and send him out that few extra yards. This exercise should be repeated no more than another couple of times, ending the day with the dog still fresh and interested.

Be sure to master the above stage thoroughly before putting out a third and fourth dummy. The idea of using a series of dummies (strung out in a straight line over a considerable distance) is simply to teach your dog to respond to your signals by moving out in a fairly straight line and continuing to move out, without further commands, until he reaps his reward in the form of a retrieve. Now you will understand my point earlier about never fooling your dog. The amount of confidence he now has in you will be a major factor in determining the success of this enjoyable but often frustrating exercise.

Some dogs learn to follow your foot scent to the dummy. Do not be concerned about this at first, but if your dog begins to do this fairly constantly, eliminate the scent trail by using a field that has a track running along its outer edge. By walking along such a track (before bringing the dog out) and throwing the dummies out into the grass at regularly spaced intervals, creating in doing so a line of three or four, you will cut out that direct line of scent from one dummy to the next. This may confuse the dog for a short while, but diligent use of the stop whistle and hand signal should help him to catch on.

The dummy launcher can once again be of considerable help by enabling you to stand at a fixed point and fire out two or three dummies, each of which can be directed to fall at a different distance by using light, medium, or heavy charges.

A slight variation on the method I have described above is one I use from time to time with retrievers while walking them to heel in the fields. I take with me a training dummy or a dead pigeon in a pocket or bag and surreptitiously drop the object behind me and walk on thirty or forty yards. I then turn, *hup* the dog, and send him. Repeating the exercise I gradually increase the distance until blind retrieves of some considerable length are being accomplished easily.

The logical next step is a blind retrieve across a creek. Precisely the same method is employed—but with just one dummy or pigeon.

10

Housing Your Dog

OPINION VARIES AS to whether an adult gun dog or a potential gun dog puppy should live in its own kennel or in the house. I hold one firm opinion: Compromise! Have your dog in the house part of the time and in a kennel for the remainder. I have always believed it to be essential, if you hope to get good responsiveness from your dog, to keep the dog in the house with you for at least part of the day. A pup isolated in a dog run with little human contact will often develop temperament problems. It may well develop a fear of people. It may in fact develop a fear of *anything* that it has not been given the chance, while young, to become familiar with. To suggest that keeping a young gundog-to-be in the home will ruin it is nonsense. Provided that common sense is exercised and nothing stupid done (such as allowing the pup out to wander and hunt on its own), nothing but good will result. At the same time however, it is good for a puppy or an adult dog to have a home of its own, i.e. a kennel-and-run. Dogs like having a place they can regard as their own.

I certainly think that a kennel-and-run is preferable to what I consider the very undesirable method of chaining a dog to a small doghouse. I believe that being tethered and consequently severely restricted can have detrimental psychological effects.

If lack of room prevents you from constructing a kennel, don't be concerned. Keeping your pup in the house with you all the time will be fine, and no adverse effect on his hunting ability will result. Don't believe anyone who tells you otherwise.

THE DOG RUN

For the owner with just one dog, setting up a kennel-and-run will present little difficulty. First you will want to choose a location, and in making this decision the main thing to remember is that dogs prefer even sub-zero weather to extreme heat. So pick a section of yard or garden that is shaded during the hottest part of the summer.

I suggest that the run for one dog be not less than six feet wide, six feet high, and twelve feet long. If you like you can use four-by-fours to make frames—six-feet-square each—on which a good-quality two-inch mesh-welded wire (which comes in rolls six feet high) can be stretched. Then each section—including a gate frame—can be bolted together so that the run can easily be taken to pieces should you ever have to move it.

I recommend, however, that you consider ordering a run from one of the many kennel manufacturers. You will get a complete run delivered in sections of any dimensions you require and made of galvanized steel piping with the wire already stretched and secured. The package will include a gate and the whole thing can be bolted together by metal clamps in about thirty minutes.

Furthermore, the mail-ordered run is metal and cannot be chewed. It can be quickly and easily taken down. It is not unattractive, and will last many years if properly looked after. And if a second dog is acquired later, three more sections of the same type of run (back, side, gate) are all you'll need to make an additional run, as the sections are designed to clamp right on to the side of any existing run of the same size.

A small two-dog complex with roofed runs and individual houses.

Custom-made runs secured to the end of a barn, with entrances from each run to individual kennels and sleeping boxes inside the building.

A professional kennel. Ten runs outside corresponding custom-made kennels and a central corridor within. There is room for the same number of runs and kennels along the far side of the building.

THE DOG HOUSE

With the type of run I have recommended, two types of dog-house can be used as follows:

(a) The run can be secured to the side of an existing barn or shed. If this is done, the back section of the run will not be required. An entrance twelve inches wide and sixteen inches high should be cut into the building close to the ground to allow the dog access from the run. To this entrance can be fitted a two-way swinging "dog door" to help cut down on draft. Inside the building a second run, made from exactly the same type of frames, can be set up to correspond to the width of the run outside. For the inside run I suggest a wooden bed three feet square with raised sides six inches deep and wooden blocks beneath it to raise it two or three inches off the floor. Next, a box two-feet-six-inches high should be made (without a base and large enough to fit snugly over the bed). Into this box should be cut another hole at the end furthest from the dog's entrance into the building

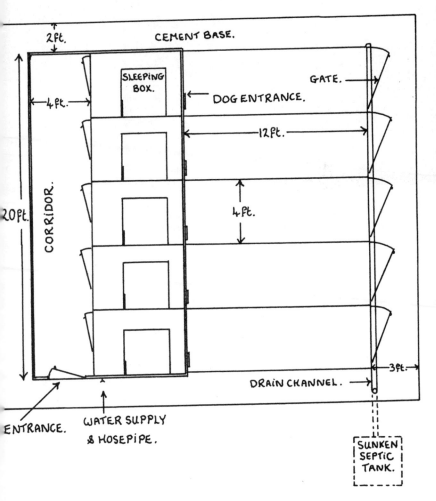

2 ft.

CEMENT BASE.

SLEEPING BOX.

DOG ENTRANCE.

4 ft.

GATE.

12 ft.

CORRIDOR.

20 ft.

4 ft.

3 ft.

DRAIN CHANNEL.

ENTRANCE.

WATER SUPPLY & HOSEPIPE.

SUNKEN SEPTIC TANK.

MULTI-KENNEL AND RUNS

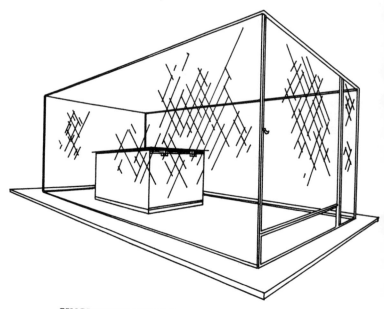

SINGLE RUN AND DOG HOUSE ON CEMENT BASE

itself. This box is the sleeping place, and the idea of the loose top is that it can be lifted off for periodic washing and disinfecting.

You now have a good draft-proof dog house within the building itself. This inner house, when filled with cedar shavings or good clean oat straw (not hay), will be ideally warm and dry for the severest of cold weather. In spring and summer no bedding of any kind is necessary. You will find in fact that your dog will more often than not use the top of his sleeping box, or even the run itself to sleep in during the warmer weather.

The bed and the box to fit over it can be made of good five-eighths-inch plywood. Exterior ply will not be necessary as the box will be permanently inside the building.

(b) If no existing building is available, a dog house can be made to stand inside the run—or purchased ready-made from a manufacturer. (We will presume that in this case you are doing the building yourself.) The plywood may be of the same thickness as for the indoors bed-and-box described above (five-eighths-inch), so long as it is of "exterior grade" and no more than three-feet square. Also, you will want to slope slightly—from front to back—to allow the rain to run off. The entrance should be located at the back and to one side and a draft board the full height of the inside of the house should be fitted (see illustration) to form a corridor with a gap through which the dog can walk to its sleeping section.

The entire front panel of the house should be made in the form of a lift-up door hinged at the top. This way the house is easier to clean and in the warm weather can be propped open to provide both shade and cool air, day and night. Again, bedding should be removed once spring arrives. Secure four-by-fours all around the base to raise the house off the ground and ensure also that the roof is either shingled or covered with good-quality tar paper held in place with wooden battens. In states where extreme cold is the norm, serious consideration should be given to constructing a dog house with insulated walls, roof, and floor.

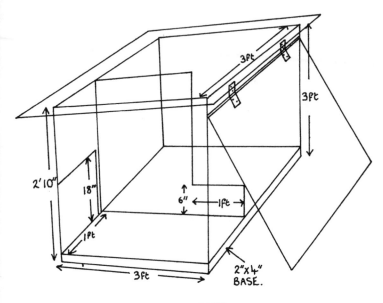

DOGHOUSE

As the outdoor house will stand inside its run, most dogs will soon learn how to jump up onto its roof. This will bring them within easy reach of the fence top, so I recommend that the run be covered with wire netting to keep the dog from jumping out (or in the case of a bitch in season, a male from jumping in). All you need is a roll of good chicken wire, as few dogs indeed would ever attempt to break through.

I think it advisable also, especially in the northern states, to have a one-foot snow panel beneath the gate. In a six-foot-high run this will mean the gate will be five feet high. Such a panel saves a lot of problems after a heavy snowfall, when a full-length gate may, under bad icing conditions, get frozen in.

RUN SURFACE

The best run surface for adult dogs is cement, despite certain drawbacks during a particularly bad winter. Cement can be hosed down and disinfected regularly and will last indefinitely. The dog run should stand free and not be cemented in, as you may want to move it some time. Two-inch-high feet are built into the custom-made metal runs so that the bottom piping stays clear of water and urine. The concrete slab should be thick enough to withstand an extremely hard frost and preferably should be reinforced with a steel mesh insert to help cut the chances of cracking. The slab should extend out about two feet beyond all sides of the run itself.

A satisfactory alternative to cement is "pea gravel," which washes well and looks clean provided you keep it replenished. The disadvantage of gravel however is that you always need a fresh supply close at hand to replace what you unavoidably threw out when cleaning the runs.

Earth runs should under no circumstances be considered as they get terribly muddy in wet weather and also harbor worm eggs much more than cement or gravel does. Thorough cleaning just isn't possible with an earth run, and as a result disease is more likely to be constantly present.

A hose pipe with a good strong jet is essential for washing down. Droppings, no matter what the surface, should be re-moved at least once but preferably twice daily. (If a dog is exercised at a regular time daily he will get into the habit of rarely fouling his run.)

A pail of fresh drinking water should always be available. This I hang by a double-ended snap-catch to the wire. Galvanized pails are fine for spring and summer, but the rubber agricultural type should be used in winter, as nightly freezing of a metal pail will crack it wide open at the seams. Solid ice can be quickly and easily freed by immersing the pail inside a larger one filled with hot water. Within seconds the ice loosens and can be thrown out. (This must be done each morning.)

I should add here that where litters of puppies are concerned, a grass surface is preferable for the first couple of months. This helps to ensure that their feet will not become splayed, as can happen if the litter is kept constantly on cement surfaces. The run that the pups are kept in should be constructed so that it can be moved daily from one area of grass to another. Otherwise the ground quickly sours due to the difficulty of removing the droppings thoroughly from the grass.

For a litter of pups I suggest a light, wood-framed run about twelve feet square with welded wire sides. It need be no more than three feet high, so that it can be easily stepped over, and should have a wooden dog house placed in it for a rain shelter. Because of their light construction, both can be picked up and moved easily by two people.

This arrangement is for use in warm weather only of course.

AFTERWORD

Paddy

THE FIRST SPRINGER spaniel we owned came to us when I was eleven years old, towards the end of World War Two. My uncle, a keen shooting man, bought the dog from a doubtful character in a pub one Sunday at lunchtime. This fellow had the dog tethered by a piece of binder twine to the bar stool and appeared to be having difficulty scraping together the few coins necessary to buy himself a drink so my uncle bought him one, his interest centered on the springer, whose appearance and temperament he was taken with. When the subject of the dog came up the man said he wanted to get rid of it due to family problems, and my uncle promptly bought the animal for what amounted to the price of a few more beers.

A lack of registration papers and the vagueness of the seller's assurances that the dog really was his raised doubts, so the matter was mentioned to the local policeman who made enquiries further afield and reported back to us later, much to my relief, that no report of the dog having been either lost or stolen could be found.

So that Sunday Paddy became ours.

In those days I used to accompany my father and uncle on local shooting expeditions on the weekends. We lived in a village in the northwest of England high up on the bleak hills which look out onto the even bleaker Pennine Moors of Cheshire and Derbyshire. There really wasn't a lot to hunt other than rabbits and a fair number of hares. Red grouse were to be found up on the moors, but the moors were private estates for the most part so forbidden territory to the uninvited.

My uncle's elderly dog "Rover," who is the first springer I can remember, died about this time. He, up to then, had been our sole rabbit finder and retriever. Now Paddy took over. We estimated that Paddy was around twelve months old when we got him and we soon found he was an enthusiastic retriever. The very morning after he arrived he picked up the newspaper and brought it to my mother, a thing he had obviously been accustomed to doing wherever it was he had originally come from.

I tried training Paddy in my own way, but of course I lacked the knowledge to be able to instill into him any real steadiness. He hunted well though and I could at least keep him within shooting distance and make him sit and stay when told—and as I said before, retrieving never was any problem as he did it naturally. He wasn't keen on water though, and it was a while before I could persuade him to retrieve from it.

The country we hunted around the village consisted mainly of small fields with hedgerows and shallow valleys along which were strips of woodland. In addition to rabbit we would get the occasional woodcock and a few snipe. Harder weather usually guaranteed we would find a few about.

Paddy's willingness to face the toughest cover was quite extraordinary. He would tear through blackberry thorns and prickly gorse for the sheer love of it and I can still clearly visualize certain bushes (now covered alas by a housing development) where he would flush out a rabbit or two almost without fail. He remembered those places and would ram his way into the middle causing the brambles to shake and heave and you had to be ready as only snap shots were possible.

Still etched clearly in my memory is the first rabbit I shot, which Paddy pushed out from nettles at the base of an oak tree on a farm we had been given permission to hunt for the first time.

As late as the late 1940s I had never seen a pheasant in my life. I used to read about them in the shooting magazines and was fascinated by the thought of the estates that were then beginning to resume rearing them (though not by any means on as large a scale as they had done pre-war).

One day in late October 1950 we were hunting some excellent woods only a few miles to the south of our normal territory when Paddy flushed, right in front of me, a cock pheasant which erupted from a bank of thick dead bracken and rocketed up through a canopy of oak and silver birch branches. I was mesmerized, but somehow had the presence of mind to lift the gun, and the bird crumpled and fell.

Watching Paddy retrieve that very first wild cock pheasant is something I shall never forget.

The availability of a car made annual autumn trips possible, and for several years we went to North Shropshire, very close to its border with North Wales, where in those days hundreds of rabbits could be seen feeding in the fields and along the hedgerows during the early evenings. Here pheasant, partridge, and duck were relatively common, and the sport we and Paddy enjoyed on those long glorious October weekends was indeed superb.

Shooting around home still took place whenever possible, and there being little in the bag was fully compensated for by the pleasure of Paddy's company.

But by now he was getting old.

The fact that infirmity was prevailing over a willing heart became painfully clear. For the last twelve months before he finally passed away, Paddy's hunting trips were dreams before the fire.

I came to realize that Paddy had, during his time with us, taught me how much pleasure there is to be gained from hunting with a good dog. His presence had enhanced every day afield for me. My interest had been in him far more than it had been in the

Paddy

shooting. It was to watch Paddy hunt, and to see him retrieve, that I had walked the fields and woods.

This interest in gun dogs—or working dogs of any kind for that matter—first awakened in me by Paddy, has remained with me ever since. And I know for certain that if I were unable to take a good dog afield with me ever again, I would have no interest in going hunting.

Those who hunt without a dog just don't know what they're missing.

Index